ISBN: 979-8-218-50442-7

Printed in the United States of America

www.AmphoraConsulting.com

The Amphora Consulting Team

Jeff Bennett

Darrin Fleming

Nick Demos

Lee Ann Schwope

Bill Braun

Foreword

In October of 2019 we both published our seminal book, *Grassroots Strategy* and simultaneously began publishing the *Amphora Consulting Blog*. Our blog topics provide practical lessons and reflections covering the full spectrum of our Grassroots Strategy framework, from Market Definition to Business Model, as well as providing general lessons for improving your business strategy and execution. At times, we simply wrote about things that were on our minds.

What you will find in the *Grassroots Strategy Reader* is the compilation of those blog posts as well as a few posts that we wrote and were published on other sites.

We have organized the content into sections that loosely map to the Grassroots Strategy process, with a few extras thrown in at the end. Feel free to skip around and choose the topics and articles that most spark your interest. The articles in each section are mostly in the order that they were published rather than any other organizing principle. We have not edited them from the original, allowing you to see that some of our predictions during the Covid era were about as bad as everyone else's.

Where possible we have provided the URLs to links that were embedded in the online version in case you want to explore those threads.

As always, please feel free to reach out to us with any questions, comments, or even critiques. Primarily we hope you will both enjoy and find value in *Grassroots Strategy Reader*.

Section 1: Strategy

Introduction

"Whatever you do, don't get trapped into a debate around the definition of 'strategy.'" We received that warning during one of our first Grassroots Strategy workshops, from an academic colleague with a long executive education pedigree. While we learned a lot from our partnership with this professor, and we deeply cherish his friendship, we did not always follow his advice.

We believe that it is essential to have a good working definition of strategy - if you can't define what a strategy is, then you don't know what you are looking for. Yet there is ample truth in our colleague's advice – 'strategy' is one of the most over-used and mis-used words in business, and yet really good strategies remain relatively rare. I suppose that is why it is a topic that we return to frequently in our blogs.

In the following, we attempt to clarify what a strategy is (and what it is not) and highlight many of the reasons why companies of all sizes get strategy so wrong. We also strive to be practical, after all a strategy that only exists as a PowerPoint document is close to worthless. For that reason, we provide some tips on how to turn a strategy into an action plan that drives real change in your business.

As always, we also try to have a little fun, drawing strategy lessons from as far afield as Irish Pubs, African tribes and super-heroes. Enjoy!

Now that you have an annual plan, do you really have a strategy?

December 11, 2019

It's the holiday season, a time of parties and good cheer and for many companies a time to negotiate and finalize budgets going into the new year.

If you are like many of our clients, you may have thought about strategy and long-term goals sometime in the late summer/early fall and probably presented something to your leadership and/or your board at that time. But then the pressures of the end of year set in and you have jumped into the more urgent process of annual financial planning and managing an overloaded calendar as you grapple with the dual challenge of making the year's numbers and negotiating the right set of resources and goals for next year.

For some of you this process is nearing completion. For many these goals are still being negotiated, reviewed and revised as well as being coordinated across departments. For others the budget has already been presented and sent back for more revenue growth or further cost cuts. With the holidays coming up it is often the case that it will not be until January that this process is compete and everyone knows their targets and budget expectations for next year.

But while all this necessary and important work is going on, where is your strategy? If it is gathering dust on a bookshelf, then how is it impacting this process? If your strategy is not reflected in the objectives and goals being set for the organization, then what do you think will change and how will the strategy be achieved? If you are asking yourself these questions, then it's probably a good time to dust off your strategy and re-frame this end of year frenzy of activity by focusing on what you really need to do to make that strategy real and win in 2020 and beyond. To do so, you might start with a series of questions that are frequently overlooked:

1. Is your 'strategy' really a strategy? A strategy must reflect a logic for how the business intends to win against its competition, the core capabilities that will enable it to win, and a business model that will allow it to grow and profit into

the future. Goals, slogans and mission statements may have their place, but they are not a substitute for strategy. Nearly all the strategic plans we have reviewed over the years have a long-term financial projection and a list of action plans. These are necessary to run your business, but not sufficient to define a strategy. Strategy is found in the 'why?' questions behind these actions and forecasts; for example: 'of all the things we could have done with our resources, why did we choose this list?' and 'why do we think it will work?' If you can't answer these questions and do so in a way that is concise and credible when communicated to your organization, then you don't have a strategy.

2. Does your strategy frame the key trade-offs your organization has to make? The difficult part of implementing a strategy is not deciding what is good (more revenue, more profit, happier customers, etc.), but rather deciding how to approach issues where two 'goods' come into conflict. Years ago, one of our clients paid another consultant to develop a new strategy for them following the merger of two companies. What they summarized and presented to the organization was: "We aim to have the most satisfied customers, most engaged employees and most productive operations." Although these are all great ideas, they fail to help when the organization is making real trade-offs; for example, I can do extra work to make this customer more satisfied, but that will take time away from other activities and hinder productivity. Or I can give every employee two weeks of training per year to improve their engagement, but that means two weeks that they are not available to respond to their customers and might impact satisfaction. If your 'strategy' does not help make real world decisions about priorities and resource allocation, then you still have some work to do.

3. Is your organization aligned with the strategy? Peter Drucker famously said, "Culture eats strategy for breakfast," and that is still true today. If your organizational structure and culture do not fit with your strategy, the strategy will lose. Every time. One of our clients built a new strategy around the differentiator that they were the only truly global supplier in a business characterized by mostly smaller, regional (single continent) companies. The

strategy made sense and passed most of our tests for a good strategy. But they quickly recognized that the organization was not ready, and further the structure was in the way. For years they had operated with region (US, Europe, Asia) as the first break in the organization chart. In fact, there was not a single function that was organized globally, and regional leaders interacted only sporadically, often just around annual functional meetings. So, while it was technically true that they were the largest global supplier, they effectively ran as three regional suppliers. Changing the organization was a necessary prerequisite for implementing and seeing the benefits of the new strategy.

4. Are you prepared to publicly make decisions based on the strategy? Your organization is not the philosopher's tabula rasa or blank slate. Anyone who has been around awhile has seen lots of announcements about new visions, directions and yes, strategies, but then nothing really changed about their jobs. So, it is rational for these people to take a wait and see attitude. Until they see a consistent set of decisions and actions visibly linked to the strategy (and demonstrably different than in the past), they are likely to perceive this as more of the same. As a leader, you should be conscious that whatever the strategy is on paper, your actions and decisions are building 'case law,' the set of precedents that over time shed light on the gray area between what is consistent with the strategy and what is not. If your leaders are just using the strategy to justify whatever they would have done anyway, then you can bet that the rest of your organization is doing the same.

A thoughtful and coherent strategy should be the foundation for not just annual planning, but ultimately execution. If your goal setting and budgeting has become disconnected from your strategy, then now is a good time to ask whether or not you really have a strategy at all. If you are going through the motions of goal setting and budgeting without a refresh of your strategy and without reference to your strategy, then you may be building on shaky ground and at some point, your results are likely to pay the price. Finding, articulating and then utilizing a coherent strategy in the sweet-spot intersection between customer needs and your unique capabilities is the only way out. If the planning cycle is coming to an end and you have a budget and a set of goals for 2020 but you don't have a strategy or a real plan, now would be a great time to finish the work to make that strategy real, positioning your business for success in the upcoming year and maybe taking some of the pain out of this annual ritual in the future.

Why do I need a Strategy if I have a Corporate Strategy?

January 19, 2020

The holidays are over, 2019 books are closed, and yearend financial results will shortly be communicated to investors and the public. The Corporate Strategy has been refreshed and will be further communicated to analysts and investors. In all likelihood, goals and budgets have also been negotiated and are locked in for 2020.

Now is the time that you can settle into running your business. You have a set of sales targets, budget requirements and maybe product launches or geographic expansions that you have planned for and committed to for 2020. But independent of all of this, do you really know what you need to focus on to win in 2020 and set yourself up to win going forward?

One place you might look to is Corporate Strategy. The Corporate Strategy provides a view to the aspirations of the company, has a perspective on the desired portfolio of the corporation and has a view of what capabilities will be maintained by the company at the Corporate level. It all makes sense to you and may put some limits on what you can do; but it doesn't tell you specifically what you should do in your part of the business and doesn't tell you how to win in your business.

Often times we have seen Business Units or leaders within businesses go through the exercise of developing a strategy by trying to conform to the Corporate Strategy of the company. This misunderstands the role of the Corporation relative to the role of the Business Unit in most companies. The Business Unit, often called a "Natural Business Unit" groups a set of activities of the organization within similar markets, with common customers and common competitor sets. The existence of the business unit is precisely to allow for the leadership closer to the customer to compete and win against their competition with a strategy specific to their markets, customers and competitive set and with decision rights and accountability to execute this strategy.

A Corporate Strategy is generally not enough. Many of the companies we work with are Corporations with several different business units or lines of business. It would be unreasonable to believe that that the Corporate Center would dictate the strategy to each of its business units or business lines, since each one is often in completely different markets with different competitive environments and drivers of customer value. Instead, the Corporate Strategy typically does the following:

1. Defines the Role of the Corporate Center Relative to The Business Units

2. Defines the Critical Capabilities that will be Maintained at the Corporate Center

3. Determines the Portfolio of Businesses that the Corporation wants to be Invested in, and sets the criteria for investments, and

4. Allocates Capital Among the Opportunity Sets

The Business Unit Strategy is very different. The business unit strategy defines how the business unit will drive future growth in profits by defining:

1. How the Business Unit is differentiated or can be differentiated versus its competitors

2. How the Business Unit will create value for the relevant customer base

3. How will the Business Unit grow revenue and profits in the relevant markets (What customer segments? What geographies? What Offerings?)

4. What capabilities are required to be maintained, developed or acquired to win and prosper in these markets and/or how will the corporate capabilities be utilized to create an advantage in these specific markets?

A portion of this may be related to the Corporate Strategy, for example if the Corporation provides differentiation and/or the business unit leverages capabilities provided by the Corporation. But typically, in a multi-division company, the Corporate Strategy does not and should not be the same as or take the place of the Business Unit Strategy. And, not all business units are created equal – some may be multi-billion-dollar businesses in their own right. In this case, more detail around the product line or customer segment strategies may be warranted.

At Amphora Consulting we believe deeply that strategy should not be a top-down exercise that is handed down to those responsible for the actual businesses. Instead strategy and strategic thinking should be a capability built deep into your organization that creates growth from each of the businesses in your portfolio through empowering those responsible to think strategically, understand how to drive customer value, and take the actions that will allow them to win against the competition within their space – what we call "Grassroots Strategy."

This requires business leaders who know the principles of strategy, know what a good strategy looks like and know how to develop a good strategy. This requires an organization accustomed to strategic thinking trained in market back strategy principles. And this requires accountability and decision rights structured to empower businesses leaders to take strategic action.

2020 promises to be a year filled with opportunity. But a corporate strategy alone is not enough to make that opportunity real. We believe you can unlock the potential of your businesses by allowing their leaders to think strategically, act strategically and drive growth for your company.

Is it time to take the 'product' out of product management?

February 19, 2020

Frequently, we are asked to tailor our 'Grassroots Strategy' workshops to serve as training for product managers. Typically, the identified need is a lack of strategic thinking and/or tools for analyzing markets in a company's product manager group. Beneath the surface, however, we believe that the problem may run deeper. The problem may be grounded in the very definition of what a product manager is and therefore what the rest of the organization expects from them. We have come to the conclusion that there are at least three different roles that can all have the title 'product managers':

1. There can be 'engineering' product managers, who keep drawings and bills of material up to date for the product line and may manage incremental product enhancements, but generally are focused on short-term customer (or sales) – generated requests, and do not have a full P&L view of their decisions. This definition is most common in highly engineered/customized products – we had one client who made huge valves for the oil and gas industry, they decided this was the only kind of product manager they needed and re- organized so that all product managers reported to a VP of Engineering (obviously, they were not very open to our 'market-back' approach)

2. Mainly in the chemical industry, especially in commodity markets, the term 'product manager' usually means someone focused on managing the supply side of the business. In the complex world of byproducts and co-products, this person determines the mix of product outputs (think about a refinery) and decides what to upgrade and what to sell on the raw market. This person generally owns the Sales and Operations Planning process (S&OP), and reports directly to a business unit leader (i.e., it is not 'sales' or 'marketing' or 'operations' but a distinct and separate discipline). This person usually has responsibility for a range of products defined by a set of assets (for example, all European

refineries), rather than a set of end-use markets.

3. Sometimes called a 'product marketing manager', there is often a person focused on the market for a given set of products. This person typically owns SKU management, product launches and at least a high-level pricing strategy. They also usually oversee, or at least approve, marketing communications for their products. Sometimes this role is compared to the Brand Manager in consumer products, who oversees and directs a brand without having solid line responsibility for Sales, Operations or R&D.

Depending on your industry, one of the first two types may be necessary. But we think it is almost always a mistake to overlook the third definition. Someone needs to be looking at the market beyond current requests from customers and thinking about what we should offer in the future, not just 'how' do we do it today from a technical standpoint.

To make this role successful, we have identified a number of key factors:

- First and most important, this person must be responsible for overall product line profitability and growth and so must be able to see the impact of their decisions on both the cost and revenue side of the income statement. If product line P&Ls don't exist, you will need to create them, no matter how much kicking and screaming there is from accounting. Keep in mind that these 'shadow' income statements need not be perfect to be highly informative.

- Second, this person should own (and be able to defend) the product roadmap, clearly articulating the priorities for new product development, and the segments we are targeting. In addition, they should understand how these new offerings will create an advantage – what are the customers' alternatives and why do we think we can win against them?

- Third, this person needs to spend significant time with customers, not asking about 'satisfaction' with current products, but looking for unmet needs – problems that we might be able to solve in the future.

- Fourth, this person must be able to see beyond the product to think about alternative ways to solve the customer's problem whether they be in-kind competing products or seemingly unrelated software, subscription services or alternative business models.

In addition to these specific abilities, it is critical to find and develop product managers who can balance the short- term and the long-term; responsibly dealing with the business and customer issues of today, while creating time to be proactive in helping shape markets for offerings that may not exist yet. P&Ls are essential, but if hitting profit targets becomes the only measure of success this could lead to a very short-term orientation. Therefore, some additional metric or metrics are required to measure market share, health of the product pipeline, or some other leading indicator.

Doing all this well is not easy, the internal focus on products and the short-term tactics they drive (price lists, brochures, trade shows) comes with deadlines and can too easily crowd out the longer term thinking and analysis. In our work, we are absolutely convinced that the underlying skills can be trained. But we are equally convinced that the skills will atrophy if they are not reinforced routinely by the rest of the business, especially other mid-level managers. These managers and their leaders should stay close enough to distinguish those product managers who 'get it' and are making the right trade-offs from those who are sacrificing critical investments in order to achieve short term targets.

Changing expectations Is necessary to make these kind of product managers truly effective and ultimately drive a culture change to a market (not product) led organization. To underscore the importance, about 3 or 4 years ago, one of our clients replaced the term 'product manager' with 'offering manager' to signal both that it was not just a product-centric role and that the desired outcome was a complete offering to solve the customer's problem, not necessarily just a product.

If your product managers don't know what is expected of them and are not thinking this way, maybe it is time to get them away from their products and out into their markets. The tools and frameworks in "Grassroots Strategy" are a great place to start.

Not-for-Profit is a Tax Status, Not Your Strategy

February 6, 2020

In our consulting careers, we have worked mainly with for profit organizations – businesses varying from start-ups to fortune 500 firms. In fact, most of you reading this probably work primarily in the for-profit sector, although many of you may serve on boards or otherwise volunteer for nonprofit organizations outside of work.

It is in this context that we are asked from time to time if our 'Grassroots Strategy' framework applies in the nonprofit world. After some reflection and a couple of attempts to make it work, we are convinced that it does work. However, we have come to realize that nonprofits frequently need to add an additional step at the beginning of their strategy discussions.

In retrospect maybe it should have been obvious, but we take it for granted that the ultimate goal of most of our clients it to make more money – a goal usually measured as return to shareholders. Therefore, strategy is about understanding customer needs and differentiation in order to choose the right initiatives to achieve that objective. For nonprofits, where the goal is explicitly NOT to make a profit, the goal is rarely as clear. Consequently, we have come to realize that the first step in effective strategy for not-for-profit organizations is agreeing on the metric you will use to determine success.

Before we come back to this important difference, let's review some of our '**universal truths about <u>strategy</u>**' (https://videos.files.wordpress.com/4miV3AwD/02_whatisastrategy-jeff-v2_hd.mp4) and how they still apply at nonprofits:

1. *Strategy is about choice, particularly choices where reasonable people can disagree* – just like in the for- profit world, articulating what you will NOT do is one of the tests of whether or not you have a strategy. Further, setting quantified goals too early (we want to raise $3 million more than last year), while it may motivate fundraisers or members, can actually hinder a real discussion of strategic choices.

2. *Strategy is about the allocation of resources* – it should be obvious for nonprofits that you can't do everything – you have limited resources. And exactly like for profit companies, spreading your resources too thin will just make you mediocre at lots of things, generally not a winning strategy for either achieving your mission or fund-raising

3. *Strategy requires an honest look at the momentum of the business* – This means asking tough questions about how we got here and why. Are we growing as fast as similar agencies? Why is our membership declining? Without a good understanding of the forces that got us here, we are unlikely to figure out how to change the path.

4. *Strategy must change the decisions that people make* – As a nonprofit, you most likely have a vision or mission statement, but is that really driving the decisions that people make? We would argue that this aspect of strategy may even be harder for non-profits. Especially for those organizations dependent on volunteers, deciding to stop funding someone's pet project can be an unnatural act.

5. *Done well, strategy is hard work* – While we firmly believe that strategic thinking is a teachable skill, part of our success with corporations is that our audience shares a common language to describe their business and at least some have heard many of our terms before in business school or prior training. This may not be the case at a nonprofit where many of the key decision-makers work directly in the field and have limited backgrounds in business.

As if wrestling with these challenges is not difficult enough, as we've already hinted, there is an additional question that non-profits have to answer before they can even begin: how will we measure success? You probably have some sense of what you want the organization to achieve, but is your view the same as other leaders/board members? Further, have you boiled it down to a metric that can be tracked, or are you forced to settle for an 'I'll know it when I see it' definition of success?

The importance of this was driven home the first time we tried to engage a non-profit in a strategic discussion as a board member of a regional child services organization. The management presented a strategic plan that was a thorough and insightful examination of the environment coupled with some financial projections by major service. It reflected a great working knowledge of the areas in which they practiced and was generally well-received by fellow board members.

When we started to ask a few questions, however, things quickly unraveled. In particular, management had only partial answers to questions about why the agency was investing in some areas and not others. We came to realize that the problem was not management, rather it was inconsistent direction from the board. Specifically, the stated mission of the agency was to 'get every child into a safe and permanent home' (paraphrasing).

However, many of the board members were operating as if the goal was simply to have a bigger budget than the previous year.

This turned out to be a critical distinction – while private, and with a foundation built by some very generous and involved donors, the agency received most of its operating income as reimbursements from the state and county welfare authorities (through Medicaid and a handful of other programs). The reimbursement rates varied depending on the type of service with the very highest 'per child' rates being for children with severe behavioral issues that needed full-time, 24-hour supervision and could not be safely introduced into an adoptive home.

Maximizing revenue would have meant housing as many of these children as possible and keeping them on-site for as long as possible. In contrast, if the goal was 'permeance' as the mission implied, the agency should focus on investing in early intervention, refining techniques for working with parents and children so they never got to the point where they needed institutional care. Said differently, the agency would be most successful by working itself out of existence in an admittedly unrealistic world where every child was born to parents with the desire and capability to raise them.

In another case, we worked with a membership organization for business leaders facing high turnover in their member base. When we first asked about measures of success, the immediate response was 'number of members.' But after some discussion we helped them realize that it was not that simple. Advancing the organization required engaged members, not just members on paper, and the members had to have the right background and be at the right level at the right companies to have an impact. In the end, we agreed that something like 'companies with engaged members as a percentage of the total target market' was a more complete description of what we were really after.

These examples highlight the particular challenge for nonprofits, as often there is no easy answer for a single metric. But if all you have is a list of lots of things that are good, it is not helpful when making trade-offs among multiple 'goods' or competing attractive-sounding options. While there is no universal formula, a few guidelines have begun to emerge:

1. Engage the organization (and probably the board) in this discussion – even if it takes a while to get to a consensus, there is value in the struggle; and especially if there are opposing views, huge value in just starting the dialogue.

2. Be creative in developing a measure, even if it is not perfect, and even if does not exist – in our example above, the children's services agency might have begun to look at number of days until permanent or something similar, even though that would be influenced by changes in the condition of children at intake and may not have been previously measured

3. Don't be afraid to 'think like a business' – while many in the nonprofit world may shy away from managing 'by the numbers,' in the end you have limited funds and can only do so much good. Don't you owe it to your constituents to understand what is most effective?

4. Ideally, agree on a metric that will help allocate resources – for example, these two initiatives require the same budget, but which will be better for the agency? Without a metric of success, this question is

entirely subjective, and the temptation to do a little bit of both may be overpowering. But if we can develop the equivalent of 'return on investment' it can be quite helpful in making these tough calls

We wanted to leave you with one final thought. Many in the nonprofit world may be suspicious of the profit motive and generally distrusting of 'shareholder value' as a measure of success. In a sense they are right, not-for-profit enterprises are serving a higher mission. Their 'stakeholders' voluntarily parted with their money and/or their time because they believed in the cause. They are not some distant Wall Street speculators, but rather the very communities in which you operate. Therefore, it is imperative that nonprofit leadership sees to it that their stakeholders' resources are put to the best possible use. Defining how you measure success seems like pretty good starting point.

Strategy, Focus and the Perfect Pint

March 12, 2020

In 1759, Arthur Guinness leased a disused brewery in Dublin and began producing beer for the local market. Like most brewers of his time, he produced a variety of beers to meet a variety of tastes. But by the late 1770's, Guinness was becoming known for his porter. The dark beer that used roasted barley to produce a deep brown color and rich complex aroma had become quite popular, especially among the dockhands in Dublin. In 1799, faced with a shortage of capacity, Guinness made the bold decision to discontinue production of his various other ales and focus exclusively on the porter – the beer we know today as Guinness Stout.

This historical tale underscores one of the most powerful and difficult challenges of strategy – focus. Remember that strategy is about choice and that strategy starts with understanding your differentiation – being able to leverage the small number of things (capabilities or strategic assets) that you can do systematically better than your competitors. Conversely, if you try to do everything, you will spread your resources too thin and very likely not be the best at anything. This is why a strategy has to be more than just a roll-up of department-level improvement plans.

This simple truth seems obvious, but can prove extremely difficult for companies, because focus means not doing some things that might seem attractive. Focus means placing bets – a focused portfolio is less diversified and that can make some managers uncomfortable. And focus means killing some projects that may still have fans in the organization or among your customers. For example, there must have been some Dubliners who preferred the taste of Guinness' other, long-forgotten brews.

In our work at Amphora Consulting, we help clients overcome this by concentrating not on what they can do, but what customers want them to do. From the critical and objective view of the market what really differentiates their offerings? Where can they truly be the best in the world, and which customers value this difference? That is the essence of what we call your strategic 'sweet-spot.'

Importantly, focus does not mean giving up on growth and innovation, it just means being more disciplined about where you look for adjacent opportunities. Again, the Guinness story is instructive: in 1901, Guinness built its first technology center to advance the science of brewing. Throughout the 1950's Guinness was at the leading edge of transitioning to stainless steel and aluminum brewing vessels to improve quality and consistency, and in 1959 they introduced the dispensing process still used in pubs today utilizing nitrogen in addition to carbon dioxide to produce a consistent creamy head.

In 1988, Guinness introduced the 'widget,' a patented packaging system that allowed the experience of Guinness Draught to be enjoyed in a can – delivering the same combination of gases to the beer as the can was opened.

After seven generations of family ownership, Guinness PLC was sold to Diageo in 1997, and today Guinness customers enjoy more than 10 million pints per day in more than 150 different countries.

So, the next time you celebrate the end of a workday with a proper pint and admire its perfect one centimeter of dense creamy foam, consider the power of strategic focus and the lasting impact of understanding and building upon differentiation. What could it mean for the future of your business?

Source: *Guinness Archive, GUINNESS STOREHOUSE®, St. James's Gate, Dublin 8; as well as significant personal research*

Are You Ready to Come out on Offense?

April 24, 2020

With all the major sports leagues shut down, perhaps it is more important than ever that we keep alive that grand American business tradition – the sports analogy. So here it goes boxer Mike Tyson once said, "Everyone has a plan 'til they get punched in the mouth." At this point in the Covid-19 crisis, which sums up where most companies are with regards to their 2020 plans – we are reeling from being punched in the mouth.

Our hearts go out to all those who have lost loved ones, and our thanks to those who have been risking their lives on the front line fighting this invisible enemy. As we write this, there appears to be a light at the end of the tunnel, people are making plans to re-open the economy. But to Mr. Tyson's point, those can't be the same plans that we had coming into the crisis. You've been punched in the mouth, what do you need to change before the bell rings to start the next round?

The current situation is unprecedented, at least in our lifetimes. There is literally no one alive who remembers a global pandemic of this magnitude. That being said, we can and should still learn from history. While no two events are identical, from the long view, there appears to be some kind of macro event that reshapes the world every ten to twenty years or so. While unforeseen, these shocks cause structural change such that the world coming out is fundamentally different than the world going in. Our list of these occurrences includes:

- World War One (US involvement 1917-1918)
- Spanish Flu Pandemic (1918 – 1920)
- The Great Depression (1929 – 1939)
- World War Two (US involvement 1941 – 1945)
- Civil Rights movement (culminating in the late 1960s)
- Oil Shock/Energy Crisis (1973 and again in 1979)
- Oil Shock/Global Recession (1990 – 1991)
- September 11 attacks (2001)

- Financial Crisis (2008 – 2009)
- Covid 19 Pandemic (2020 – ?)

And that is just a partial list of calamities. We've left out many other dramatic events with huge, localized impact and often global ripple effects (think, fall of the Berlin Wall). These events differed in important ways, and there is no single parallel to the current situation. Yet, what do these events have in common? As a species, we survived, we recovered, we generally even thrived. Human beings in general, and Americans in particular, are very resilient. Yet in each case, the 'after' was different than the 'before.' Government regulations and people's attitudes changed, often in ways that were hard to predict. For example, soldiers returning en masse from World War II with a boost from the GI Bill, which helped many of them go to college and buy houses, fueled a booming middle class that no one could have imagined in 1939. Many things that had been luxury products (or pure science fiction) like televisions and dishwashers, were soon commonplace in working-class American homes.

So, what can you do now? If you have made the tough decisions to get through what could still be several more dark weeks, and are thinking about what comes next, here is our advice:

1. **Develop a perspective on what changes will be temporary and what will be permanent**. Will more employees working from home become the 'new normal'? And if so, what will that mean for the demand for office space and therefore office furniture? On the other hand, what could it mean for videoconferencing services and the infrastructure for reliable bandwidth? How might these changes and many others affect your customers?

2. **Understand that not everything will bounce back at once**; It is becoming clear that we will see a staggered restart to the economy – by state, but also by sector. As restrictions are lifted, end user attitudes may depress demand for certain products and services. Sure, you may run out immediately to get your hair cut, but are you in a hurry to book a European cruise this summer? Will your customers come roaring back,

or proceed with caution?

3. **Update your understanding of the end-customer**. We have long argued that the foundation for a good strategy is an understanding of customer value at all levels of the value chain. But how is that likely to change? Too many companies focus on what we want (sell more of what we already have, preferably at higher prices) and not what the end-customer really should want – objectively, what is their best option, given their trade-offs and limited resources? If you can't answer that question about your customers, now would be a really good time to invest in that understanding – how will your customers, and their customers, lives and problems be different?

4. **Understand your strategic assets** and be creative about new ways to pivot and drive customer value. At times like this, it is critical to unpack your strategic advantage and think about ways to re-package to create new opportunities and perhaps even new business models. For example, Panera Bread has started selling groceries: bread, bagels, milk, yogurt and even fresh produce at many of its stores. This is not just a panicked response to a decline in sales, but rather a clever way to leverage some of their core strengths: baking bread on site and managing a perishable supply chain, to meet the changing needs of a customer base trying to leave their homes less often – instead of buying a sandwich, buy the ingredients to make yourself a week's worth of sandwiches. How might you recombine your strategic assets to better serve your customers?

5. **Plan with an eye towards the option value of your position**. As you make the difficult decisions about what to cut and what to keep, do so with an eye towards the future – what will best position you for a range of possible futures? For example, food delivery service Postmates is paying their drivers a premium to keep working through the crisis and yet has waived their consumer delivery fee (they still charge some fee to the restaurants for whom they deliver). They are betting that for some time, home food delivery will remain a popular option and that they can be a

preferred partner – already on everyone's speed dial, creating switching costs that will be hard for competitors to overcome, even when sit-down restaurants return in some form.

Remember, hope is not a strategy; we can't assume that things will soon be just like they were before, and we can all breathe easier. Military planners call this trap 'preparing to fight the last war.' The most famous example is the French preparation prior to World War II. Recognizing that the Germans were ramping up their military in the 1930s, the French built up massive fortifications along the 'Maginot line' – the front across which much of the severe fighting in World War I took place. They failed to acknowledge what the Germans had learned from their loss in WWI. Having no desire to get bogged down in lengthy trench warfare again, the Germans developed the concept of 'Blitzkrieg' – audacious concentrated attacks led by armored divisions that could cover tens of miles in a day. Using this tactic, the Germans invaded Belgium, rolled through the Ardennes, and got behind the French lines, thereby experiencing relatively little resistance between them and Paris, and forcing a quick French surrender. How have your customers and your competitors adapted to the 'war' that is to come as markets open up?

To wrap this up with another sports analogy: Legendary DePaul University basketball coach Ray Meyer led his team to 21 post-season appearances in his 42 years at the helm (1942-1984). He was famous for saying that the most important part of a basketball game is the first two minutes of the second half. To paraphrase his logic: given three or four days to prepare, any decent coach can get his team ready for an opponent. But at half-time you have less than 20 minutes to revise your strategy and effectively communicate it to your team. More importantly, you are not just planning to face the team that showed up in the first half, but anticipating the changes that the other coach is making in their team's locker room. In short, that is where coaches earn their keep.

So, when the whistle signals that play can resume, how can you be ready to come out on offense, and not be stuck on your heels?

Co-written with Don Gottwald, an advisor, investor, and consultant based in Carmel, IN https://www.linkedin.com/in/dongottwald/

Kenny Rogers on Strategy

June 1, 2020 on thoughtLeaders.llc

When my sons were about 6 and 8 years old, in an effort to create an alternative to video games, I taught them to play poker. Okay, so that admission probably disqualifies me from any 'father of the year' awards. But in the process of watching them learn to play, I gained some fascinating insights both about how novices approach poker and, by analogy, how many companies appear to approach strategy.

It didn't take too long for my children to get a grasp of the basic rules and hand rankings (three of a kind beats two pair, etc.), but even with this working knowledge, they weren't very good at the game. What I realized is that without an intuitive knowledge of probabilities, they were focused only on what was possible, and not what was likely. This caused them to rack up big losses because they would keep betting on a bad hand long after an experienced player would have folded. In short, they hadn't taken Kenny Rogers' advice in The Gambler: "you've got to know when to hold 'em and when to fold 'em..."

When I asked them to describe their thinking, it was something like: "I will stay in, because if the last card is an eight, I will have a straight and will likely win." Whereas an experienced player would have looked at the same cards and said: "I am going to fold because if the last card is anything other than an eight, I will have nothing and will certainly lose." My children were focused on the possibility that the outcome they desired would occur, whereas the experienced player is thinking through the probability that it will occur relative to other possible outcomes.

It occurred to me that on a grander scale, this is a problem many companies face with their strategies and goals – they tend to hold onto a comfortable direction that might work, rather than thinking more objectively about the risks of the current course and what options might be more likely to work in a competitive and dynamic market. This should be the essence of leadership – decision-making in the presence of risk. Yet, why is it that so many companies get this wrong? We believe there are several reasons:

Internal focus

Too often companies define their strategies in terms of what they want (e.g., "we want to shift our mix from products to higher margin services") without an adequate understanding of the customer value proposition (why will customers pay us a premium for these services given their other alternatives?). As a result, too often, the bulk of a company's precious time with customers is spent trying to convince them to buy what the company wants to sell, rather than listening to what customers really need.

Inertia

At too many companies, "we've always done it that way" is an acceptable (and often unspoken) logic for business plans, and questioning this can be seen as a lack of support. It may feel more comfortable to keep betting on the hand we have and hope that this is the year the market turns around or customers fall in love with our service, rather than save some of our chips for another bet where the odds may be more in our favor.

Overconfidence bias

Many business leaders are naturally confident and optimistic. This is likely an essential skill if they grew up in sales, where you have to treat every call like it is going to be the next big deal; but it is counter-productive when thinking about strategies. There are too many variables we can't control, and false confidence about staying the course may cause us to overlook more attractive opportunities elsewhere.

Lack of awareness of tools/frameworks for strategic thinking

Everyone knows how to make a financial projection look good in a spreadsheet, but is there a strategy behind it? In our experience, too few companies work to broadly teach strategic thinking, leaving big parts of the organization executing largely on autopilot until a new strategy is delivered by "someone else". In other words, it's not sufficient to learn the rules of poker, someone needs to teach you how to play the game.

So how do companies get around this in their strategic planning? We have a few suggestions:

Focus first on what customers want, not our internal goals and objectives – if we can find a customer problem that we can solve better than anyone else, we can get paid to do so, even if we can't project exactly how much or how fast. If your team has not practiced listening to the real voice of the customer, this is a great place to invest in outside resources to teach them the basics of market insight.

Separate the strategy discussion from annual business planning – a focus on financial projections will naturally lead to a focus on only those known opportunities that feel comfortable and that we can commit to with some degree of certainty. Often strategic planning runs right into annual planning, leading naturally to a target negotiation process. We suggest running strategy on a completely separate timeframe – if you haven't done it for a while, why not start now?

Create a safe space and/or workshop where we can talk objectively about how we got here and what may be changing with customers and competition – it is also necessary to acknowledge the risks of sticking with the status quo. You might think about devoting part of your next off-site meeting to an honest discussion of the momentum of the business – what forces got us to where we are, and given market trends and challenges, what is likely to happen if we do nothing fundamentally different? This can be a great way to surface and socialize the unspoken risks of a 'try harder' strategy.

Take the time to train your organization how to think strategically. This will help them understand that confidence in a strategy comes largely from a process of elimination – yes, this direction might not work, but it is more likely to work than anything else we have yet thought of; in other words, it is our best bet. This also requires acknowledging the risk of complacency – at some point, failing to change may be the riskiest course of all.

Finding a way to have this dialogue and embedding this type of strategic thinking in your organization is not easy, but it is possible. It is precisely what we have been doing with our 'Grassroots Strategy' sessions over the last 16-plus years.

To finish the poker story: as my sons began to learn how to think about probabilities, their skills improved dramatically; though sadly, not enough to overcome the allure of video games. But we still play from time to time, and they more than hold their own. Like even the best players, they will never win every hand, but they are a lot better at knowing when to fold and how to bet when they have a potential winning hand (bluffing will have to be a topic for another day).

In the end, that is about what we should expect from a strategy: not guaranteeing that we never lose, but rather objectively assessing the situation in order to help us to recognize the limitations of our current hand, know when to stop certain initiatives and how to place bets that improve our odds of winning. In addition, this upfront acknowledgement of risk should help us think about natural 'off-ramps.' Strategy should not always be a 'bet the farm' moment; rather we can define smalls steps and interim measures of success where we can evaluate and 'pivot or persevere' based on early feedback.

If your planning is mainly a financial exercise based on hopeful sales projections to meet a top-down revenue growth target, then you haven't incorporated these critical strategic concepts, and you may be drawing to an inside straight. This might work for a while, but as a reckless poker player inevitably finds out, it will eventually catch up with you. Before you double down on your current hand, it may be a good time to objectively assess the odds. As Kenny Rogers also said, "If you're gonna play the game, boy, you gotta learn to play it right"!

Note: Kenny Rogers died at his home in Sandy Springs, GA on March 20 of 2020, at the age of 81. The great man may be gone, but his music and his wisdom live on.

"I know it when I see it"

January 20, 2021

Defining strategy so your organization can soar.

We had this difficult conversation with a client CEO recently:

Amphora: *We are having a hard time getting anyone on your leadership team to articulate your strategy.*

CEO: *Why do they need to know?*

Amphora: *We would think that strategy should be guiding their decision making.*

CEO: *My team understands that we win by being first to market with new product features and delivering best in the category of customer support.*

Amphora: *Yes, but no matter how great those new product features are, they eventually get copied and margins start to go down.*

CEO: *Right, so then we have to find the next feature or customer segment where we can win.*

Amphora: *And how do you do that?*

CEO: *Well, we've always been able to do it before.*

Amphora: *And what will the next opportunity be?*

CEO: *I don't know today, but I'll know it when I see it.*

Many mid-sized companies become successful based on the intuition and experience of the CEO (often the founder) and sometimes one or several members of the Senior Management Team. Oftentimes they understand particular customer problems well and have developed offerings that uniquely solve these customer problems. Growth in the business comes from growing the customer base within their target segment and expanding their share of wallet among customers in the target segment by expanding the scope of the solutions.

The company is served well in this model because through history and experience the management team has developed an empirical understanding of what works and what does not. Over time, through hard work and sometimes trial and error, they refine these understandings and can be extremely effective and successful driving a business based on the experience base and understanding of the CEO and/or core Leadership Team.

However, as companies grow to a certain size this approach to running the business is often no longer sufficient:

1) The company's success leads it to expand to the limits of the customer set and scope of problems available to it, further growth is outside of its "intuitive strike zone". 2) The company becomes big enough that the resources of the core Leadership Team become strained by the sheer volume of decisions to manage. 3) and sometimes, there is a market disruption (new technology, new entrant) such that the experience and intuition of the management team no longer reflects the current market realities. It is in these circumstances where a well- articulated strategy becomes an important tool to augment the talent of the CEO/Leaderchip team.

It is true that there are counterexamples of larger companies that have been guided by visionary CEOs who have intuitively connected offerings and customer needs in ways that revolutionize markets. But these are few and far between (usually in B2C) and 'it has always worked before' is no guarantee that it will work in the future. Even the genius of Steve Jobs which brought us iTunes and the iPhone, was also responsible for the Lisa, the Newton, the Apple III and the long-forgotten Pippin gaming system.

So, companies above a certain size eventually need to articulate their strategies, not just have it in the leader's head. This is the premise that led to the name of our book, "Grassroots Strategy." Specifically, we believe that good ideas can come from anywhere, so with more people looking for the next opportunity you are more likely to find it. At the same time, not every idea can be turned into good business, so you need a framework to guide and evaluate this ground-level strategic thinking. In fact, this is one of our definitions of strategy: "a framework for allocating resources that produces more than the sum of marginal decisions."

It would seem to be straight forward to explain the strategy of the business yet in our experience many companies still struggle creating a well-articulated strategy. We believe there are a number of reasons:

- First, strategic thinking requires a different skill set than instinctively running a business. Just like the best players often make horrible coaches because they cannot articulate what seems like second nature to them in a way that is helpful to others, the same is true for many entrepreneurial leaders.

- Second, as companies mature or change ownership, there is a natural tendency to focus on financial outcomes. "Our new private equity owners want to double EBITDA in four years" may be a good objective, but it is NOT a strategy.

- Third, for many entrepreneurs, the idea of focus can be scary. Focus means ruling out options, declaring things that you will not do. This can sometimes feel like it is constraining and consciously or unconsciously, some leaders fight it.

- Fourth, many company leaders believe that their business and their strategy is too complicated to explain to others (perhaps even including their board and some of their functional teams) Yet in our experience, if you can't explain your strategy, you probably do not really have one. We are reminded of the 'mother-in-law test': if you can't explain what you do in words that your mother-in-law would understand, then maybe you don't really understand it yourself.

- Fifth, declaring a strategy for others to execute may feel like a loss of control. Many entrepreneurs whom we have met have an amazing capacity to remember details – reminiscing about every customer interaction, the way you remember the milestones in the life of your own child. Delegating some of this interaction and judgment to others can feel

30

like a personal loss.

When business leaders explain to us that, "they will know it when they see it," we can't help but be reminded of the famous quote by Supreme Court Justice, Potter Stewart writing in 1964 on determining whether a movie was obscenity or protected speech, "I know it when I see it." Just like that decision was a cop out that has led to decades of legal decisions constantly redefining that boundary, it is inadequate when it comes to a definition of strategy.

To be successful at the next level, executives have to learn to articulate their strategies – getting them out of their heads and onto paper, so they can become tools for the rest of their organization to adjust and improve. While not exhaustive, below are some thoughts that might help in this transition:

- Recognize that the essence of strategy is choice – specifically how will we make trade-off decisions where reasonable people might disagree. Developing a framework that clarifies what we will do and what we won't do, and why this might be different from our competitors' view, can go a long way to clarifying your strategy.

- Don't get overly focused on objectives – yes goals are important but setting financial targets too early in the process can actually inhibit strategic thinking, or worse create distractions and inefficiency to meet some arbitrary goal. Your strategy should be built around making the most of the hand you have been dealt, not meeting some arbitrary quantified goal.

- Understand that you can't please everyone – allocating a few resources to every plausible idea may seem fair, but it is likely far from optimal. Picking the handful of initiatives that are most likely to succeed and doubling down on them may not make everyone happy, but it is almost always a better way to maximize results.

- Live the strategy – recognize that every strategy has some 'gray area' and how you make decisions around these boundaries will form the 'case law' that impacts how your organization interprets the strategy. Not long ago, we were working with an industrial equipment company on a strategy to shift scarce technical resources to new product development and away from supporting low margin legacy products. Specifically, they decided that supporting the nearly 50-year-old Model 400 series products was on their 'won't do' list. About two months into the roll-out of the new strategy, a customer called and wanted technical support on their Model 400 machine. Not wanting to say 'no' to a customer, the CEO relented – technical resources were diverted and their strategic initiatives suffered. Worse yet, the organization learned that it is ok to work on Model 400 machines as long as a customer asks, putting the credibility of the entire strategy at risk.

As we have said elsewhere, for these reasons, doing strategy well is hard work. It requires stepping back from the unrelenting pace of day-to-day judgments and practicing a different way of thinking. It requires exploring what could be, not just the customers and opportunities that are visible at the moment. Yes, it can be difficult and lead to some awkward conversations. But in our experience, it is almost always worth it.

Further, strategic thinking is a learnable skill – just because an organization has not lived through a real strategy exercise before does not mean it is impossible. With grounding in our "Grassroots Strategy" principles and a little coaching, organizations can make tremendous progress, creating a strategy that aligns the organization, focuses resources, and accelerates results.

Strategies to Stand the Test of Time

February 8, 2021

Is your strategy precise or robust?

Precise: "*Exactly or sharply defined or stated*" (Merriam Webster Dictionary) or "*Marked by exactness and accuracy of expression or detail*" (Oxford English Dictionary)

Robust: "*Capable of performing without failure under a wide range of conditions*" (Merriam Webster Dictionary) or "*Sturdy in Construction*" (Oxford English Dictionary)

It is with some optimism that we are beginning to look forward to a not-too-distant future where we can eat in restaurants with no restrictions and only medical professionals wear masks. It may be a good time to start making plans again to replace the cancelled gatherings, concerts and vacations we have missed over the last year. More to the point, it might also be a good time to revisit your strategy with an eye towards how markets and customers have changed and approach the future with some humility about how little your dated projections from 2019 resembled what actually happened in 2020.

Hence our question, "Is your strategy precise or robust?" – we have long felt that the goal of planning should be to produce strategies that are robust, not precise. Yet too often strategic planning is inseparable from budgeting and long-term financial planning where the output is expected to be detailed revenue and profit projections by product line or by geography by quarter.

Financial projections and expectations are, of course, important. But it is equally important to make sure the is robust across several potential future scenarios and anticipate financial outcomes across these different scenarios. It is also important to be clear about the assumptions behind the strategy: what market information should be tracked in order to adjust the strategy over time, what you should expect to see if the strategy is working and what might indicate that it is not working and therefore trigger a reconsideration of the strategy. The problem is that in the quest for precision ("the numbers have to tie"), the disciplined thinking that is needed for robust strategies can be lost.

Forgive us for a brief digression into the difficulty of making precise predictions.

Can you fill in the next number in this series: 83, 28, -8, 38, 24, 86, -9, 4, ? This is not a sample Mensa test question, rather it is the annual growth rate (in percentage points) in electric vehicle sales in the US going back to 2013. Yes, sales actually fell in 2019 vs. 2018, and despite a horrible quarter due to coronavirus shutdowns, EV sales were up slightly for the full year in 2020. So, what will they be in 2021? I am certain you can buy a report that projects EV sales to increase at 23 percent per year – but do they give you a confidence range? History suggests that the confidence range should be wide, including the possibility that sales may fall before rising again. We might generate a financial projection assuming EV sales will increase at 23 percent per year, but it would foolish, some might even say dangerous, to base a strategy on this precise expectation.

Strategists cannot get away with blindly accepting some expert's projection of the future, nor is it reasonable to assume that the future will look exactly like the past. So how should you incorporate uncertainty into your strategic planning? We've written previously on the importance of thinking through what is temporary versus what is likely to be permanent and the importance of thinking through second and third-order effects. For example, if half the people working from home continue to do so, what does that do to the demand for office space and the commercial real estate market? Not to mention the demand for office services or office furniture?

Beyond that, as you refresh your strategy in these turbulent times and strive to avoid the precision trap, here are a few thoughts to keep in mind:

- It seems obvious but make your assumptions explicit. If your strategy is predicated on something like 'everyone knows that oil prices will keep going up,' but you have not stated that explicitly, you may not react quickly enough when prices actually fall.

- In general, don't plan for a point estimate of the future, better to understand the drivers behind the observed trends and how sensitive your intended direction is to changes in them – for example, how much of the fluctuation in electric vehicles sales was due to macro-economic trends vs. the impact of tax incentives and subsidies, or the popularity and prices of individual vehicle models?

- Use ranges of estimates to test the robustness of your strategy – e.g., "if this market is 25 percent smaller than we think it is, is launching this new service still a good decision?"

- If there are multiple major either/or type assumptions (this new regulation goes into effect or it doesn't) consider scenario planning as a way to prepare for multiple futures, ideally avoiding the debate of how likely those future scenarios may be.

- Identify the key indicators that your assumptions are wrong and try to build in an early warning system to trigger re-visiting your strategy – in fact, during times of great uncertainty, more frequent strategy refreshes seem like a best practice, even without specific outside triggers.

- Lastly, it may seem counter-intuitive, but when there is great uncertainty, it may be even more critical to be explicit about what you will NOT do. Responding to the unanticipated requires flexibility and forces difficult trade-off decisions. Clear guardrails are an indication of a robust strategy. And the more robust it is, the more it can guide these tough decisions without time-consuming approvals and allow your organization to respond quickly to the unexpected – for example, a twenty-fold increase in the demand for personal protective equipment.

As Heraclitus said more than 2,500 years ago, "The only constant in life is change." Yes, much of what we experienced in 2020 was unprecedented. And while no one could have anticipated all of the events and ramifications in detail, those companies with robust strategies have done the best job of making the fast pivots required to survive and thrive and will come out on top.

Separating your strategy process from financial planning and embedding the idea of robustness as opposed to precision will help you weather the next storm. Because however much we don't know, we can predict with certainty that this will not be the last crisis.

In search of …… silver bullet strategy

April 12, 2021

Too often, companies believe that the purpose of strategic planning is to find some magical 'silver bullet' that will solve all their problems and guarantee a path to profitable growth. A frustrating conversation with a client we had a few years ago comes to mind:

Amphora: *What do you think of this draft strategy?*

Client Executive: *I don't know, it feels like something is missing.*

Amphora: *Well, is there something wrong with our logic? This strategy should result in higher growth and higher profits.*

Client Executive: *No, but it's based on information we already know, I was looking for a big idea.*

Amphora: *Yes, but this strategy is completely different than how you currently operate; it clarifies the underlying business trade-offs and forces different choices. Is there something you think we overlooked?*

Client Executive: *I just feel like there should be something more, like an outside-the-box idea.*

Amphora: *Is there any specific big idea that you think we should investigate?*

Client Executive: *I thought that was what you were going to come back with.*

Expecting your strategic planning team to come up with the next big idea to guarantee profitable growth is a bit like asking for a plan to lose weight without diet or exercise, or a plan to make money in the stock market without taking any risk. It would be nice if these strategies existed, but it is rarely the case.

Our experience is often the opposite – strategies are not about one big idea, rather they are a coherent set of actions grounded in a clear vision of your differentiation and how you can use it to win. The best strategies are based on defining your unique capabilities and aligning your business model around

36

customer segments who value those capabilities. In our experience few companies do this well but when they do, the results are impressive.

Occasionally, this process produces some pretty big ideas. We've said elsewhere that we have a fondness for strategies that are 'just crazy enough.' If a new strategic direction doesn't sound a little crazy at first, it may be that you are just describing what you do today, or worse, what everyone else in your industry is doing (of course, a strategy can be too crazy, if it requires technology that doesn't yet exist, for example). But even these 'just crazy enough' strategies need to be grounded in your current situation and capabilities. If you are launching a new offering, or if your industry dynamics are changing, it may be a great time to consider changes in your business model, changes in pricing mechanisms or assumption of risk in ways that had been previously overlooked or dismissed. Selling 'power by the hour' is a well-known example of an idea that sounded absurd to many when it was first considered.

On the other hand, sometimes the best strategies seem obvious in retrospect: "of course that is our strategy, given who we are and the market opportunities available to us. Why wouldn't we pursue this strategy and why would we allow ourselves to be distracted by other "opportunities"?" This doesn't mean that a strategy is right just because it is comfortable; the underlying logic should still be robust. The process of articulating and pressure- testing your strategy may seem like hard work, and it is not as sexy as finding the next big idea, but it is usually far more effective.

If you are confused about the goal of the strategy process, there is also the risk of 'dressing up' a small idea to make it seem like a big idea in order to satisfy the strategy gods. Some may remember something called Efficient Consumer Response (ECR) that many packaged good companies pursued in the 1990s. The allegedly big idea was to get the product from the factory to the consumer as efficiently as possible, which leaves one wondering what the previous idea was. Too many companies used ECR as an excuse to spend millions on distribution and IT projects without addressing the root causes of the current inefficiencies, much of which was due to bad promotion policy ("loading the trade") and had nothing to do with IT infrastructure. And, by calling ECR a

37

"strategy," some companies overlooked opportunities to create real winning strategies grounded in differentiation.

Yet this quixotic quest for a silver bullet strategy persists. Why is this? We have assembled a partial list of reasons:

- **Hope triumphs over experience:** It is enticing to think that there might be a quick answer that would solve most of your problems. As evidenced by the continuing stream of fad diets that produce best-selling books, the hope for a quick fix can overcome logic. In the business world, these quick fixes not only rarely work but can have major unintended consequences. We recall one client who cancelled all their distributors to pursue a direct sales model and two years later was trying to re-sign distributors after this strategy fell on its face because their previous distributors picked up competing product lines and largely retained their customers.

- **The grass is greener:** Sometimes the hope for a silver bullet is also fueled by the 'grass is greener' syndrome. We know all the difficulties and challenges of serving our current customers, if we could just penetrate this new market, everything will be fine. Again, this is rarely the case – the new market almost certainly has demanding customers and entrenched competitors that you just can't see from the outside.

- **Everyone else is doing it:** We also find that the blind adoption of some big idea is more likely when 'everyone else is doing it.' Just like buying the latest diet book, some companies adopt the latest management fad and assume that it is a substitute for strategy. Adopting something like lean or agile may be a good idea, but if everyone else is doing it, by definition it is not a differentiator. Pursuing these goals may help the company improve, but at the risk of strategic drift without a proactive direction in the market.

So, what is a company to do to avoid this trap? Well first, clearly define what a strategy is. Strategy is about providing a framework for the choices you make that distinguishes what is good business for you in contrast to your competitors. Strategy is hard work, but there is no way to short circuit the basics:

- Be honest about the momentum of the business – how much of previous success was your company and how much was the market?

- Force your team to articulate what problem we solve for a clearly defined customer. Saying that everyone along the value chain is a customer may sound good, but it may also sidestep critical trade-offs that lead to important insights. When you can't make both the distributor and the end-customer happy, whom do you choose? This is a good way to break out of "we've always done it this way."

- Be brutally honest about your differentiation – what is its source and what is it worth to customers? If you have trouble identifying real differentiation, be honest about that as well, and turn your attention to where you could differentiate with focused effort.

- Look for sweet-spots where your differentiation solves (or could solve) a customer problem, ideally an unmet or under-met need, and clearly define the customer segment that has these needs.

- If possible, think about the potential for a business model flywheel that makes your differentiation more valuable and sustainable over time. What can you do with today's customer to build scale, knowledge and/or capabilities that make you more valuable to customers in the future?

The result may not be the "big new sexy idea", but if your logic is sound, it should be the roadmap to growth, profitability, and enhanced shareholder value. Coordinated action in a consistent direction will pay dividends: choose the right bait and drop your line in the right spot and you will catch more fish. In business, like in life, sometimes the big new sexy idea is that there is no big new sexy idea.

So, stop searching for the next fad diet and get on the exercise bike. It may not be fun or glamorous, but in B2B markets having the right strategy based on an understanding of customer value and a powerful needs-based segmentation of the market can lead to sustainable competitive advantage and that is actually pretty cool.

Do you Prefer Superhero Strategy Lessons from DC Comics or Marvel?

July 1, 2021

When we were kids (yes, we had cars and televisions back then), there was no doubt that the DC universe of superheroes was cooler than the Marvel Universe. DC had Batman and Superman, the two coolest crimefighters, plus we had the Justice League cartoons on Saturday mornings and Lynda Carter's Wonder Women on TV. DC Comics (yes, we bought them occasionally) attracted better artists and had better story lines. Marvel Comics, in contrast, seemed childish and sometimes downright silly (remember Shazam!).

But clearly things have changed – today there is absolutely no doubt that the Marvel Universe is cooler. In fact, it isn't even close. So, what was it? How did Marvel overtake the DC heroes we knew and loved and leave them in the dust? Scanning the internet, there are a surprising number of opinions (ok, maybe not that surprising), but we have distilled it down to six key themes, all with implications for how you should think about your business strategy.

1. At least in the cinematic version of its universe, Marvel has an organized and planned sequence of movies that links storylines and characters. While each movie stands on its own, the connections reward the avid viewer and enrich the development of what otherwise might be overlooked characters.

   - **Strategy lesson**: Strategies need to be coherent and coordinated in their implementation – a bottom-up list of improvement plans is not enough.

2. Marvel has kept its characters up to date as the audience changed. Classic heroes like Iron Man and Captain America have been creatively reimagined in ways that engage younger audiences. DC has been less effective, with its key heroes still rooted in original stories that date to the 1930s.

   - **Strategy Lesson**: Strategies need to be revisited as markets and customers' needs change. Don't be afraid to break from what has worked in the past.

3. Marvel has a wider variety of characters targeting different demographics and attitudinal segments. In contrast, DC has focused mostly on Batman and Superman, trying to stretch their classic do-gooder image for broader appeal, but with limited success that recently resulted in a few truly awful movies (Justice League, Batman vs. Superman).

   - **Strategy Lesson**: Don't try to straddle segments. If you want to target more than one segment, you need to do it with different offerings.

4. In general, Marvel characters have better back-stories. In many cases, this makes the characters more human and therefore easier to relate to. In fact, as far back as the 1970's, Marvel characters were described as more 'naturalistic,' having human emotions like tempers and bad moods. With the possible exception of the Wonder Woman movie, DC has struggled to bring anything new to its well-known origin stories since we learned that Jack Nicholson's Joker was the street thug who killed Bruce Wayne's parents in the very first modern Batman movie (Michael Keaton, 1989).

   - **Strategy Lesson**: Don't forget that strategies need to motivate people. Strategies that connect to a clear and compelling purpose will be more likely to succeed.

5. Marvel movies have generally done a better job of injecting humor, sometimes in generally light-hearted films like Antman. But there is often a humorous theme even in more serious movies – think Thor with a beer gut in Avengers: Endgame.

   - **Strategy Lesson**: Don't take yourself too seriously. You can't know everything about your market or about the future, yet at any given point in time, you need to make strategic choices. If you get it wrong no one dies. And if you are monitoring your strategy appropriately,

41

you can typically course correct before too much is lost.

6. Finally, we can't ignore that, up until his death in 2018 at age 95, Marvel had the unparalleled genius of Stan Lee. Not only was he the creative force behind nearly all the great Marvel characters, but he was also able to imagine the unifying canvas that brought them all together and defined their interactions (and make his famous cameo appearances). DC characters, on the other hand, generally were invented separately and evolved apart, only coming together for 'corporate events' like the Justice League which always felt a bit artificial.

- **Strategy Lesson**: First, as we've said elsewhere, cherish your polymaths – that artist working in the corner sketching Spider-Man may actually have a broader vision to redefine your category. Second, while strategy should be communicated broadly, strategy should probably have a single owner to coordinate various inputs and initiatives and ensure that the output is a coordinated set of priorities and actions. You can't count on strategy coming together magically at a once a year off-site.

When it comes to strategy, it should be clear that you can't rest on your past success. You may feel like Superman today, but a chunk of Kryptonite is never too far away. Companies that continuously revisit their strategies and have the courage to question previous assumptions and potentially even disrupt themselves will succeed and become the Marvel universe of their industries. Those who fail to adapt risk waking up to find that their superpowers are no longer relevant.

Don't Wait for the Perfect Mission and Vision Statement to Create a Strategy

August 2, 2021

We often talk with companies who are waiting to work on their strategy because they are reworking their mission and vision statements. There are key differences between mission, vision and strategy and it is essential they all fit together to drive impact. Successful companies connect these three pieces together to ensure their business focus is clear, communicated and market driven. But strategy is too important to be put on hold while you search for the perfect mission and vision.

Employees and customers can be genuinely inspired if their organization has a clear, worthwhile mission and a compelling vision. The key is knowing the difference between these statements and a strategy. A mission statement should provide purpose to the entire team, defining what makes your business important. A well-articulated vision statement will inspire your team and customers to a future state of impact. Typically, the founder or executive leadership team is responsible for describing this future state. This aspirational view should open the door for employees to feel purpose at work and customers to want to work with you, however it does not substitute for a strategy.

A market-back strategy doesn't start with aspirations or quantifiable goals. Rather it starts with understanding customer value and then on identifying differentiation or potential differentiation that allows your company to deliver customer value and so drive growth in your business. Strategy is a clearly articulated view of the distinctive capabilities that allow you to win in the relevant markets and presents a framework for management decision making that creates outcomes that are more than the sum of marginal decisions. Strategy has to be more than 'everyone try harder' – it is the roadmap for what you will do and what you will not do, helping the organization focus its resources and maximize their return. A well-defined strategy can have an enormous impact on your business with or without mission and vision statements, it isn't something you should ever push to the side or delay.

We call the intersections of what customers should want and what you are uniquely able to provide, your "sweet spots". When you focus business decisions on your sweet spots, you can drive growth, ensure you don't become a commodity and keep your team focused on value versus fluff. Articulating value from the customers' perspective is critical, as what customers pay for is actual improvement in their business, not marketing spin.

Customer value is always: customer specific, measured in currency, and relative to their next best alternative. Thinking that your mission and vision statements create value by themselves is a dangerous trap.

Our advice: Make sure you don't put your strategy on hold while updating your vision and mission statements. To drive results, focus on working these core components of your strategy to set you and your company up for success.

1. Understand the Momentum of the Business: Have a clear and objective understanding of your business and how you got there. Was it a well-defined plan or was luck involved? How is the current state going to impact the business in the coming years? Without a good understanding of the forces that got us here, you are unlikely to figure out how to change the path.

2. Define your Sweet Spots: Your sweet spots are found at the intersection of what the customer should want and what you are uniquely qualified to provide. Having a clear understanding of under-met needs combined with the core competencies you are ready to provide creates clarity on where you should focus your limited resources. This is grounded in being able to think objectively from the customer's perspective, not biased by our hopes or ambitions.

3. Identify your target market segments: Find groups of customers with similar underlying needs and define your value proposition. Our detailed blog on "Market Segmentation: How to Get it Right" outlines a few things to keep in mind as you work as you work through this critical task.

4. Become a student of your customer: Good VOC is not a customer satisfaction survey, rather it is the ability to genuinely put yourself in their shoes and understand how they make decisions – this is the only way to uncover unmet needs.

5. Execute, Review and Refine: A well-done market back strategy has a clear plan to execute but also reviews client feedback and refines as necessary. This includes defining up front the measures you will use to track the strategy. This is critical to distinguishing problems with execution from problems in the underlying strategic thinking and it ensures that you can keep your market back strategy current as markets and competitors change.

Once completed you can ensure your market back strategy (strategies) are in line with the future state articulated in your vision statement and is in support of your mission statement. Strategy work should never be put on hold and can be done before or in parallel to the development of your mission and vision statements.

Make Sure You Don't End Up With a "Paper Strategy"

January 27, 2022

The last two years have been pretty crazy. Whether your business has been doing well or badly in this environment, much of the last two years have probably felt a lot like crisis management. Starting with the new year in 2022, it's a good idea to refocus your efforts on achieving your long-term strategic goals instead of continuing to just react to the short-term chaos. At this time of year, most companies already have a strategy in place. Hopefully, this strategy has at least informed your annual budgets and financial targets for the year. But have you thought about how to balance the short term need to 'make the numbers,' with the long-term actions needed to make the strategy real?

At Amphora we are a boutique consulting partnership focused on developing impactful strategies for our clients. If you have read our book, "Grassroots Strategy: Cultivating B2B Growth from the Ground Up", or worked with us to develop your Business Unit or Corporate Strategy, you know that we have well-formed views on what a good strategy is and a proven process to develop one.

Typically, developing a strategy is structured as a discreet project; however, finalizing the strategy document is obviously not the end of the process. The strategy needs to be implemented, monitored and adjusted over time. A strategy is explicitly about making decisions today focused on achieving a result in the future. As we often say, a strategy that doesn't change the decisions that you make is unlikely to be a good strategy. If you do not plan what you will do to achieve your strategy, set aside resources and define specific milestones, you are unlikely to achieve the desired future results.

Several years ago, we worked with a mid-sized company to develop a strategy for the business. The management team, the board and our team believed that we had developed a winning strategy that would deliver outstanding long-term growth and set the company up to be a leader in their industry.

One year later, we were asked by the board to come back and revisit the strategy. After some examination we determined that the company had delivered earnings beyond expectations but had not grown relative to their markets and had not really done anything but pay lip service to the strategy we had developed together. In a discussion with the board, we all agreed that the strategy was still the right strategy but that the management team had not done anything to implement it. One of the board members put it best, he said "So you mean we have a really good strategy on paper and now we need to turn it into a real strategy".

Since we judge ourselves on results, we felt at least partially responsible and dug in to see what we could do to turn our 'paper strategy' into a 'real strategy.' It wasn't too hard to figure out that higher than forecast commodity prices that year had provided the business with great tailwinds that allowed them to easily make and exceed their earnings targets, almost completely explaining the performance. Like most companies, the management team was primarily compensated on earnings and the quarterly board meetings focused mainly on updates versus the plan, with strategy relegated to an annual discussion.

To be fair the company had just come under new ownership, so they were still working out their governance model. We were able to help them establish a meeting cadence and compensation scheme that helped drive the right discussions. That having been said "paper" strategies are all too common.

At another client we were brought in to develop strategies for each of the corporation's three major Business Units. Our instinct was to start the strategy work by revisiting the previous strategies. It turns out that they had done a similar exercise three years before, developing strategies with the help of a major consulting firm, which were then presented to the board. One of the first signs that there was something amiss was the time it took for each of the business units to locate and send to us these previous strategies.

Upon examination the previous strategy work was coherent and had good ideas about how to grow the business, but apparently had no relationship to what the business units actually did over the three previous years. In fact, the business unit leaders clearly had not referred to the strategies over the ensuing three years and struggled to see their relevance now. Once again, they were 'paper strategies' documented to satisfy the board, so the management team could go back to business as usual with day-to-day operation of the business. As we helped develop the new business unit strategies, we also changed the review process to build in accountability for actually changing the business.

So how do you make sure you end up with a "real strategy" and not just a "paper strategy"? We don't have all of the answers, but we have some guidelines based on our experiences over more than twenty years and hundreds of product lines, business units and corporations.

1. **Don't "give" a Management Team a Strategy.** Strategies are most likely to be understood and implemented if they are developed by the management team themselves. Good strategy consultants can guide the process, do a lot of the analysis, make recommendations and even write the document but the management team has to make the key decisions and own the strategy itself.

2. **Don't Focus on a Document for the Board.** While it may not seem that way at the time, it is really important that the strategy be a living document that articulates how the management team intends to meet its aspirations not be framed up as something to deliver to Senior Management or the Board. The most important output of a strategy process is an agreement among the management team as to how the business will win, a communication of this understanding to the rest of the organization and a translation of this into priorities that cascade through the business. This can be reported to Senior Management or the Board, but the process should not be focused on "the document".

3. **Include Quarterly Milestones and Non-Financial KPI's in the Strategy.** Once the strategy has been developed, go through the process of being explicit about what you will start doing, what you will continue doing and what you will stop doing. It can be helpful to articulate the major "themes" or "pillars" of the strategy. Then, you can break the strategy down into key initiatives that support each pillar and set milestones for making progress against each initiative. Don't just include financial metrics, develop KPI's that reflect what we should expect so see if the strategy is working (e.g., "Version 2 of our maintenance platform

being used across the company by the end of Q2").

4. **Monitor the Strategy more than Once a Year.** Too often the rhythm of governance is dominated by reviews of financial metrics usually focused on meeting quarterly earnings goals. When this happens management's focus is exclusively drawn to the short term and it should be no mystery why, at the end of

the year, little progress has been made towards longer term strategic goals. We see the value and necessity of monthly financial and operating reviews; however, these need to be counterbalanced with a cadence of similar meetings focused on the strategy and strategic goals. In our experience these meetings need to be set up completely separate from the monthly operating meeting so that the short term does not constantly crowd out the longer-term initiatives. We think a quarterly review of progress against the strategy is about right, and if desired, a simple "red/yellow/green" dashboard can keep management informed between these meetings.

5. **Create Incentives that include Strategic Goals not Just Financial Metrics.** We are not compensation experts, but we know enough to understand that people's behavior is driven by what they are rewarded for. Compensation based primarily on annual financial results will drive short term focus. Balancing incentives between financial results and strategic goals will get a different result. If you're having trouble keeping the management team's focus on longer-term strategic goals, you may want to look at your compensation structure to make sure this is not part of the problem.

It is not always easy for strategy consultants to admit that implementation and follow-through are at least as important as the strategy on paper. But in the end, we are reminded of the Seinfeld episode where Jerry has made a reservation for a rental car, but the rental car company had run out of cars. Jerry says, "You see, you know how to take the reservation you just don't know how to hold the reservation". Developing the strategy is not enough, you also have to know how to pursue the strategy.

Do You Know the Momentum of Your Business?

February 9, 2022

When we run strategy workshops with clients, we usually start with a discussion of the momentum of the business. Borrowing from the concept of momentum in physics, this is our attempt to capture the trajectory of the business – where it is likely headed in the absence of any change in strategy?

This foundation is critical as it is the honest starting point for any refresh of strategy. But it is amazing how often it is ignored or overlooked as clients personalize success, focus on internal goals and inadvertently assume that the future will continue to look like the past.

A story from one of our clients illustrates the point. The company was a highly successful supplier of a technical sub-system that was critical to the performance of an automobile engine, impacting both efficiency (fuel economy) and emissions. They were a European company and had a near-dominant position on diesel drivetrains for Europeans OEMs. The business was successful and had grown rapidly while maintaining high profit margins (not an easy trick selling into the automotive market).

The reasons for this success were four-fold: first, the European car parc was growing; second, the percentage of new cars sold that had diesel engines was growing, driven by regulations and tax incentives in many European countries; third, the penetration of their subsystem within diesel drivetrains was growing as it dramatically improved drivability and fourth, they had a patented innovation that made their technology particularly well-suited for diesel engines.

While many at the company were aware of these market forces, they were not reflected in their long-term plans. Like many companies, their financial projections were based on improving prior year performance – "we will continue to grow at a similar rate and continue to expand margins," as any attempt to suggest that this might not be possible was dismissed as 'sandbagging.' Worse yet, the company let these financial goals guide strategic decisions, most impactfully underinvesting in technologies for gasoline drivetrains where their proprietary technology was less applicable and hence their margins were lower (meaning that winning more gasoline programs 'diluted' margins, even if they represented incremental revenue).

The outcome was almost inevitable – no trend stays a straight line forever and market forces are no different. In this case, new car sales declined during an economic downturn; the shift toward diesel actually reversed as regulations emphasized emissions not efficiency which favored gasoline; the penetration of their technology slowed as it approached one hundred percent of diesel vehicles and their technical advantage was all but eliminated when a key patent expired.

All of this was predictable, but none of it was anticipated until it was too late. When revenue and margins started to fall, the company turned to gasoline engines (where the penetration of their technology was still increasing) as a source of growth, but found themselves at a significant disadvantage, as their systematic underinvestment in gasoline products had left them with a performance gap versus competition. Despite lots of effort, the company was unable to reverse what had become almost a freefall and finally turned to bankruptcy reorganization as the only way out.

What this long cautionary tale highlights is the importance of objectively assessing the momentum of your business and incorporating that perspective into your strategic planning. Getting this right requires a commitment to:

- Keep asking "why?" to get to the root causes of performance, especially when things are going well – be very cautious of superficial explanations like "the people who run that division are geniuses" or "customers just love our service." These perspectives may be at least partially true, but they are rarely the root causes.

- Incorporate external factors into your assessment of performance – not just are we making our numbers, but are we growing faster than the market? If we are on a different growth path than the market, is it because of the segments we play in or are we gaining share within those segments?

- Accept that market trends will not last forever; make sure you understand the underlying drivers (regulation, commodity prices, technology penetration) not just some 'expert's' projection (that 'plastics are the future' or 'everyone knows oil prices can only go up').

- Start the strategy process outside of the budget negotiation and target-setting process, if possible, using an internal group that does not have a stake in negotiating lower performance targets to make them more achievable.

A humble look at any accomplishment forces one to acknowledge the role of luck. We may have had brilliant engineers and great insight into customer needs, but we also had to be in the right place at the right time. We have said elsewhere that asking why we are doing well while we are still doing well is one of the hardest things to do in business. But forcing yourself to develop an objective understanding of the momentum of the business and its root causes is a foundational element in building a strategy that can ultimately change that momentum.

Bringing Your Strategy to Life

July 13, 2022

Many years ago, we worked for a client in the commercial waste management business – they hauled garbage from commercial businesses and construction sites. We were called in because, despite having spent a large sum with a top-tier consulting firm for their strategy, they were stuck on how to implement it. The summary of the previous consultant's work was a strategy statement that read "in our industry, we will provide the best customer service, be the most innovative, be the most efficient and have the best people."

Following the consultant's advice, they had turned each of these four aspirations into an implementation initiative and appointed a senior leader to drive each initiative. The problem with this was quickly evident at their first steering committee meeting. No one was able to get through their initiative without presenting something that conflicted with another initiative. For example, the HR Vice President presented data that companies with the best people invest in an average of nearly two weeks of training per employee per year. The head of Operations interjected "how can we be most efficient if all of our drivers are out of their trucks and in a training class two weeks every year?" The meeting soon devolved into a shouting match.

When I learned this history, the root cause became obvious to me. If you read these blogs regularly, you will have already noticed that this is not a strategy – it meets neither of our **definitions** (http://bit.ly/AmphoraStrategy). Further, it overlooks the reality that strategy is about choice, specifically choices to excel at some things and not others. This laundry list of aspirations is broad enough to provide cover for just about any initiative but calling them 'strategic' doesn't make them good ideas (or good investments).

While this is an extreme example, we realized that this is a mistake companies make way too often: ignoring underlying trade-offs that are all too real. As Maya Townsend and Elizabeth Doty said in a recent **article** (https://www.strategy-business.com/article/The-road-to-successful-change-is-lined-with-trade-offs), "when leaders launch an initiative, their ability to achieve "both/and" is not yet proven." While great strategies are often built on pushing the limits on historical trade-offs (Toyota's success in pushing quality and cost simultaneously, for example), ignoring that these trade-offs exist undermines the credibility of the strategy.

Worse yet, pretending trade-offs don't exist leaves resolution of actual trade-offs to lower levels of the organization, sometimes just guessing at what "they" really want. In our waste management example, since the company was run by leaders who had grown up in operations and the key metrics they tracked were mostly around efficiency, regional leadership mostly acted as if efficiency was king and typically just gave lip service to the other aspirations.

In this work and others where we have helped companies make their strategies real, we have come up with a few general principles that will at least get a strategic transformation off to a good start:

- Acknowledge historical trade-offs – be honest with the organization about how trade-offs were made before and what has changed to make that no longer acceptable, for example: "we are losing customers because our customer service is unresponsive, being low cost alone is not enough to continue to thrive."

- Be explicit about how you want trade-offs to be made differently – some clients use our 'will do/ won't do' framework to communicate what is really different, like: Maybe will do: "Always leave a job site looking better than when you arrived, even if that means fewer stops that day". Won't do: "Accept jobs before confirming that we can fully meet delivery expectations."

- If possible, strive for a structural solution that puts trade-offs in a different part of the organization, with more relevant information. One of our clients in the equipment rental business discovered that their individual branch managers were using price discounts, sometimes for even the smallest customers, to keep up utilization of equipment. From a broader perspective, this was sub-optimal, as a branch across town might have demand to rent the same piece of equipment at list price. To address this structurally, they took all pricing authority away from branches, programing the system so they could only book new business at list price and requiring all discounts be approved at the region level.

- Over-communicate what is changing and why. Too often, leaders view communication as a one-way street. The reality is that without a safe time and place to ask questions like "why are we doing this?" and "Why didn't we consider this?", doubt in the strategy is not overcome it is just driven underground, waiting to rise up and say "I told you so" at the first little hiccup in implementation

- When deciding on exceptions, leaders need to be very conscious that they are developing the 'case law' that will determine how the strategy will be interpreted going forward. In fact, early on, leaders may even want to write opinions like supreme court justices to explain why they made a decision and the limits on how far their logic can be extrapolated. Human nature is clear, if actions don't match the words, your people will make stuff up to fit the actions, and your original intentions may not survive.

- Lastly, course correct when presented with new information. Trade-offs by nature change over time, as now information becomes available you can usually update specific initiatives and goals without discarding the entire strategy.

Oh, the waste management client – after confirming their aspirations were still valid, we brainstormed a set of options. We acknowledged that there were some very real trade-offs that could not be ignored. For many of these the individual route driver was the only person with the information and perspective to make these trade- offs, for example: "should I slow down and talk with this customer because they might want to buy an upgraded recycling program, or do they really just want to talk about last night's football game?" Efficiency would generally trump the football chatter, but innovation and customer service would say the recycling upgrade conversation is worth having – ONLY the driver can make that decision.

Armed with that perspective, we set out to design a system where drivers would be measured not just on efficiency measures (like stops per day), but instead by the profitability of their route – in other words, they would make the trade-offs as if they owned their route. We were convinced that this would lead to better customer relationships, more innovative ideas bubbling up from the field, and ultimately, attract and retain better people because the role was now more inherently rewarding (yes, you still had to haul a truckload of garbage, but most of the time you were solving real problems for customers).

Sadly, the good news ends there. Before we could pilot the new concept, our client was acquired. The new parent was financially motivated to justify their investment and so doubled down on the efficiency metrics. At least one of the local managers we had gotten to know made a point of calling to say, "I told you efficiency is all they really care about."

Happily, your story does not need to end this way. Once you have articulated your strategy, your work is just beginning. Being honest about history, acknowledging trade-offs and clearly communicating what is different are necessary steps in making implementation successful.

Your Organization is Hungry for a Strategy

November 8, 2022

We recall a rather depressing conversation with the CEO of a medium-sized company several years ago. We were trying to stress the importance of articulating a strategic agenda when he effectively shut down the conversation by asserting, "we have a three-pronged strategy: operational efficiency, organic growth and acquisitions. People need to stop asking questions and get back to work."

Regular readers will note that this fails all of our tests for a **strategy** (http://bit.ly/AmphoraStrategy). Equally troubling in this case was how horribly disconnected this perspective was from the way the organization actually worked on a day-to-day basis. As we got to know the mid-level managers, it became clear that while many of them were focused on short-term financial targets, they mostly tried to look busy while preserving some discretionary time so they could react to the next random move from the CEO – a couple even admitted as much over a beer.

This reinforced for us that strategy is not just something you prepare once a year for the board of directors, it is also a necessary requirement for a healthy organization. As this story illustrates, if you don't have a strategy, your organization is probably hungry for one. If you have hired competent people (not automatons) they are looking for reason in the actions your company takes. The most talented executives and managers want to understand how they might best contribute to the success of the organization. If the stated strategy doesn't provide these answers, people tend to make things up. The result is a seemingly endless stream of initiatives and a confused organization that doesn't live up to its potential.

Some signs that your organization is hungry for a strategy are:

- 'Flavor of the month' syndrome – leadership announces new 'strategic' initiatives so frequently that the organization learns to pay them lip service but not really change.

- Weary managers bounce from one of these 'urgent' projects to another without being able to show any consistent results.

- Senior leadership is constantly intervening in disputes as functional initiatives are pulling in different directions and surfacing unresolved conflicts.

- Staff are grumbling about the lack of consistent direction, speculating as to the 'real' reasons behind announced changes and left guessing what will happen next.

For too many organizations, the result is like eight-year-olds playing soccer – everyone chasing the ball and no one thinking through their position and the best way to contribute to the whole. But unlike youth soccer, where this can still be enjoyable (or at least good exercise), your employees will quickly get burnt out or check out – in either case, they will not be inclined to give that extra discretionary effort that distinguishes the highest performing companies.

To understand how to avoid this, start with our two definitions of a strategy:

A clearly articulated view of the distinctive capabilities that will enable you to win in the relevant markets

AND

A framework for management decision-making that creates outcomes that are more than the result of a series of marginal decisions

While both definitions are necessary to successfully implement a strategy, the second one is most critical in aligning the organization. To get your organization pulling consistently in the desired direction, a strategy needs to help them prioritize. People face trade-offs and so a strategy must provide a perspective on not just what is good (efficiency, growth, etc.) but how to make trade-offs amongst these goods.

If you have only a notion of a strategy, or are at a natural point to revisit your strategy, how can you achieve this clarity? There is no simple answer, but here are a few key principles:

- **Articulate your strategy** – Your strategy needs to be clear about what you Must Do, Will Do and Won't Do. Our 'strategy on a page' framework built around these categories has proven to not only align specific initiatives with a strategic direction, but to clarify expectations and force organizations to make trade-offs rather than accept platitudes. Often the most difficult part is the 'won't do' column – what are those specific things that others in our industry might do, but we will not?

- **Describe the rationale** – Make sure you can articulate the logic behind your strategy. Your organization needs financial targets, but they also need answers to the 'why?' questions that are in their heads: why did we choose that direction? Why don't we expand in Asia? Why can't we win in that segment?

- **Communicate the strategy** – It is critical to allow the organization to ask questions. Exactly how to do this depends on the size and culture of your organization, but it is critical that communication is a two-way street. If people do not have a way to get their questions answered, the questions do not go away, they just get driven underground, waiting to resurface the first time your implementation stumbles (or worse yet, provide ammunition for those factions who might even want to see the strategy to fail)

- **Walk the talk** – Lastly, and perhaps most importantly, you have to live the strategy – every decision that contradicts the strategy undoes hours (if not months) of communication. One example stands out – we were working with a company that sold production equipment for the food and beverage industry. They prided themselves on providing technical support that was capable and responsive. Their customers valued this since if their client's equipment failed, their client's line was shut down. As we worked through the strategy process, they struggled to put anything in the 'won't do' category. After much debate, it was decided that they would no longer support the 'model 400 series' machines – these specific machines were old and slow, and they had a powerful value proposition to get these customers to upgrade to newer machines. About a month after the strategy was rolled out, the company got a service call from a model 400 customer.

59

Fearing that they might lose a customer, they sent a service team out to get them back up and running. While this may have been the right decision for that situation, it served to undermine the strategy. The organization looked at not just that pillar, but the entire strategy, with renewed skepticism and went immediately back to trying to guess what leadership 'really' wanted. It was a depressing experience when we started the strategy discussion a year later, and realized that the company had made no progress at all on the strategic initiatives from the prior year.

If you are deep into your annual strategic planning process, or if you are looking ahead to the process for next year, it would be wise to keep this in mind. Strategy is not some optional exercise that can be disconnected from what the business does. Rather, done well, it is a necessary part of aligning your organization and achieving your potential. An organization without a functioning strategy is akin to what Umberto Eco said about atheists, "When men stop believing in God, it isn't that they then believe in nothing: they believe in everything."

Just like your body needs specific nutrients (even if you don't always like the taste), your organization is hungry for a strategy!

Impactful Strategy Lessons from the Maasai Tribe

September 26, 2023

On a recent bucket list safari in Africa, I had the opportunity to visit a Maasai village. The brief encounter with their culture was a highlight in a trip filled with highlights, and it struck me that there is a lot we can learn from this very different lifestyle.

You have likely seen pictures of the Maasai – the tall, lithe herds-people wrapped in their colorful blankets or *shukas* living much the way they did four centuries ago, before European nations began carving up Africa. Much has been written about their culture that they have stubbornly maintained even as global civilization crowds in all around.

To be clear, the Maasai life is not an easy one, nor should we blindly copy all of its aspects. I am sure that walking from dawn to dusk behind a herd of cattle is not for everyone – not to mention the lack of running water. Maasai children rarely attend school beyond grade five, and too often young girls never attend school at all.

Despite what we might consider flaws, there is undoubtedly much that is honorable about these very proud people – an internal consistency in their values and practices that is worthy of respect (if not downright awe). It also struck me that there are some lessons from the Maasai's success that can be transferred to business strategy.

What can the Maasai teach us about strategy?

1. The best strategies are both Simple and Elegant

   We have long argued that a great strategy is elegant in its simplicity – this certainly describes the Maasai way of life. Anyone who has ever seen a lone Maasai tribesman standing stoically with his staff against an African sunset understands the elegance. And clearly, the word 'simple' could be used to describe many of the aspects of their life.

   However, as with a good business strategy, the Maasai have found the right simplicity 'on the other side of complexity' that acknowledges the

61

realities of the world without overcomplicating execution. For example, the average Maasai family unit lives in a hut that is barely ten feet by ten feet, so not a single square foot is wasted. There are two sleeping niches, one for the parents and one for the (up to six) children. There is a small fireplace for heat, as cooking is over a communal fire. And there is a single shelf for belongings that is high enough to be out of reach of the sick goat or calf that might occasionally spend the night indoors. While unbelievably basic in our view, this simple space provides all the necessities, and with belongings easy to transport and construction time kept to a minimum, it allows for relatively easy moves, when conditions dictate.

2. Strategy and a coherent business model are both critical to success.

Maasai are often described as 'warriors,' and most of us would think twice before attacking a tribe who routinely face down lions with just a wooden spear and a leather shield. But the success of the Maasai as a people is due mainly to the superiority of their business model, not their success on the battlefield.

While technically semi-nomadic, the Maasai mostly live in small villages – clusters of small huts, encircled by fences made of sharp sticks. The courtyard in the village is the nighttime home for their herds, protecting them (and Maasai children!) from roaming lions and leopards.

Much has been written about the symbiotic relationship between the Maasai and the cattle they tend. Cows provide nutrition through their milk, meat and occasionally, blood. In addition, cow dung is mixed with straw to make traditional huts that are stronger than those made with mud alone, and cow hides are used to make shoes and belts. In fact, cattle are the primary store of wealth and source of status for the Maasai.

Less known is that Maasai also keep goats and sheep. Sheep are used primarily for wool to make their traditional garments, and goats are used for milk and meat. Importantly, the stakes are lower when guarding these flocks, so children (often as young as 10) hone their herding skills with goats and sheep before being trusted with the precious cattle.

Further, knowing that they will be in one place for six months or more, the Maasai plant and harvest vegetables to help round out their diet. Over time, this model allowed the Maasai to outlast local hunter gatherer tribes, who were much more susceptible to famine and drought. To this day, despite a lack of what we would recognize as modern medical care, the Maasai have a birth rate and child survival rate higher than many African countries. Like in business, coherence of the strategy and business model, not copying every passing fad, is the key to long term success. And like a good business model, culture is the 'glue' that allows it to survive, in this case passing it along from generation to generation.

3. Strategies should be consistent, but tactics should be updated.

As we've already said, the basic elements of the Maasai culture and lifestyle have changed little in four hundred years. However, if one looks closely, it becomes clear that the Maasai have adopted some elements of modern society that fit in their model.

For example, it is not unusual to see a herdsman with a smart phone. In fact, we saw one enterprising young man with a notebook-sized solar panel to ensure that his battery wouldn't die. A smart phone not only helps the time go by more quickly while walking with the herd but is invaluable in calling for help if something goes wrong miles from the village.

In a similar vein, some Maasai now ride motorbikes. Off-road bikes can travel easily on the well-worn footpaths the Maasai favor and can dramatically reduce the time required for a weekly run to the local market. Interestingly, the Maasai almost never drive cars, as this would require far bigger changes in their infrastructure.

4. Strategies are only as good as their assumptions.

We have always argued that strategies and their supporting business models need to be clear about their assumptions and when these assumptions change, it is time to update the strategy. In the case of the Maasai, their way of life requires access to communal grazing land. In Africa this is under attack both as wildlife parks are expanded (and actively policed) and as urban areas grow in size and population. Increasing private ownership of land limits the growth of the Maasai lifestyle and may eventually put it at risk. In a sense, the fence is an enemy of the Maasai that may prove more formidable than the lion.

Conclusion

It would be easy to dismiss the Maasai and their seemingly primitive culture as an historical aberration, one that will surely fade away as soon as their children discover television and free Wi-Fi. And yet, the Maasai have persevered, the majority of their offspring choosing to stay with the lifestyle despite its obvious hardships.

In this fast-paced world where we are often tempted to react to the latest fad or buzzword, there is a lot we can learn from the Maasai. If you ever get the chance to spend some time with these noble people, I hope you will consider it a privilege.

Bottom-up is Not Enough

January 31, 2024

We are on record as strong believers that the best strategies start bottom-up – in fact, we called our book "Grassroots Strategy" for that reason. Our experience is that the best ideas come from the front lines, the people who work day-to-day with customers and/or technologies and can see creative solutions to unsolved problems. However, for a corporation, this does not mean that doing strategy bottom-up is sufficient. Bottom-up cannot see across opportunities in the business units or fully leverage the capabilities of the corporation. Further, bottom-up strategy only works when the infrastructure and top-down leadership to support the process is in place. A recent client story helps make the point:

Our client was a small engineering and manufacturing company. For historical reasons, they were organized into five largely stand-alone business units. While there was a lot of overlap in expertise and some potential overlap in customer base, they operated independently of each other from sales through operations.

Responding to a board request to document their strategy, the client set to work. They asked each business unit to describe their growth opportunities and then quantify the profit potential and required investment. Each business unit laid out a plan to incrementally increase their production capacity and so grow the business. They then rolled up these financials and presented it as their strategy.

If you read this blog regularly, you know that we believe that having a plan does not mean that you have a strategy. In this case, some of the board members recognized the lack of strategic thinking as well and asked us to take a look. We then worked with the client to dig into the details and fill some gaps in their market understanding. Together, we came away with a much clearer strategy, but also saw firsthand the hazards of a pure bottom-up approach:

- Without clearly defining expectations for the market-back questions that each business unit had to answer to have a strategy, the process was largely about internal numbers and budget negotiation – e.g., since I will be held to these projections, how much investment do I need to feel confident that I can deliver?

- In fact, because each BU knew these would become their targets, they were focused almost exclusively on incremental growth because it is perceived as lower risk. The outcome was similar to what we call an 'everyone try harder' strategy – with resources spread proportionately to the BUs and no breakthrough thinking.

- When we worked with the client to better understand their markets, it became clear to us that their markets were not at all similar– in fact, the strategies, and therefore the levels of investment, should be quite different. In this case, ranging from a business that they should probably exit to a business where they have real differentiation that they could use against fragmented competition and achieve dramatic growth either organically or through acquisition.

- In addition, they missed a major opportunity – when we started with the customer perspective, it became clear that there was a significant segment of the market that would value an integrated offering which our client was uniquely positioned to provide – but they needed a different sales force structure to sell what would be a cross- BU offering (and no one was doing that today).

We continue to believe that strategy is not primarily a top-down exercise. We have seen too many smart people paralyzed while they wait for someone higher up to give them a corporate strategy. That being said, as the above story illustrates, there are some clear roles that corporate *can* play to both develop solid product line and business unit strategies; and *must* play to turn them into a coherent corporate strategy:

1. Corporate should define what a good strategy looks like – one of the best ways to do this is by listing the five or six key questions that a strategy must answer, as this encourages and directs bottom-up thinking (rather than shutting it down as many top-down approaches tend to do).

2. In many cases, an important corporate role is to support developing the skills within the business units to objectively understand markets from the customer-back – we firmly believe that this teachable skillset should be spread broadly throughout business units and not limited to a few enlightened individuals in a strategy department.

3. Ultimately, a corporate strategy needs to allocate resources, so corporate needs to evaluate BU strategies and direct investments to the best returns (not proportionate to last year's profits) – sharing these decisions and the rationale behind them will tend to reward clear thinking and help improve the quality of BU strategies over time.

4. A corporate strategy has to have a clear view of the corporate capability system – that small number of hard to copy processes/tools/systems that can be leveraged across the business units...

5. ...Armed with that, a corporate strategy should identify potential synergistic opportunities even where no specific business unit is pursuing them today, and then develop the business models, organizational requirements and/or acquisition options to pursue them.

6. Lastly, to make this sustainable, a corporate center has to implement and maintain an organizational model that balances the role of corporate functions versus BUs in a way that invests in the relevant capabilities, aligns with the strategy and minimizes conflict and duplication of effort.

In the end, we stand by our position that good strategies start bottom-up, but like many things in life, the real answer is not that simple. Without clarity from corporate and the right environment and infrastructure, bottom-up strategies can be precisely wrong and can never add up to a coherent corporate strategy. Finding a way to meet in the middle that leverages the capabilities of the corporation but captures the unique market understandings of the business units is key.

Enter the Matrix...the Ansoff Matrix

March 19, 2024

Identifying a winning growth strategy for your business can be one of the most difficult and often contentious activities you undertake. The allure of chasing that new "high growth" market is strong. On the other hand, the inertia to "stay the course" can feel comfortable to many. Finding a way to cut through the emotional reactions and chart a course to your best strategies is crucial.

The Ansoff Matrix

With that as a backdrop, let's visit a classic tool for guiding growth strategies: the Ansoff Matrix. In his 1957 HBR Article "Strategies for Diversification", H. Igor Ansoff introduced concepts on product-market alternatives that he distilled into what is known as the Ansoff Matrix. Born in Russia to an American father and a Russian mother, Ansoff moved to the US for his studies and obtained degrees in engineering, physics and applied mathematics before becoming one of the early stars of modern business strategy.

Ansoff's original article, while dated in many ways, is brilliant in that he foreshadows several management concepts well before they were in broad usage, for example:

- He uses the phrase 'product mission' to refer to 'the job your product is intended to do.'

- He recognizes that company evolution is necessary for long-term survival, so defining your business by product alone is inherently dangerous.

- He suggests that diversification should only be pursued if the selected strategy leverages some underlying expertise that will allow you to succeed in the new business, which feels like an early version "capabilities driven strategy."

Ansoff's matrix as it is usually displayed highlights 4 different strategies: existing product/market penetration, market development, product development, and diversification (which entails simultaneous product and market development). As an aside, Ansoff also offers vertical integration as another dimension not captured on the product-market matrix.

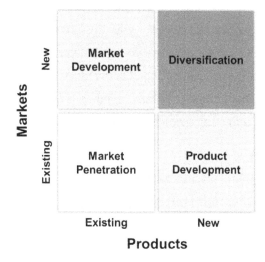

Many of our clients have used the matrix as part of their search for profitable growth opportunities. We have come to realize that, like any tool that has been around for over 60 years, Ansoff's Matrix has some embedded wisdom. But, at the same time, like any tool that has been around that long, it is prone to misuse as well.

The Ansoff matrix can be useful in the ideation process to surface new growth ideas, and it can be useful in assessing the risk of different growth initiatives. It can also be a useful tool for examining exposure to risk across a corporate portfolio. But it is only relevant with the context of the rationale for the company to seek diversification in the first place. So, it is in no way prescriptive and does little to guide the development of a strategy.

The primary failure modes we have seen in the application of the Ansoff matrix are:

- Assuming they need to have some funded initiatives in each of the quadrants (or else it will look like they are not thinking outside of the box)...

- ...Or alternatively, believing there is some optimal mix of growth across quadrants that can be pre-determined.

Somehow the Ansoff Matrix has been confounded with a balanced portfolio concept in technology management. The balanced portfolio concept suggests that R&D investments should be managed in a ratio to include business sustaining investments, incremental investments, and disruptive investments. The concept is that disruptive investments have both the highest risk and the highest reward. The confusion in the Ansoff matrix is the assumption that the increased risk as we move out of our core will also yield increased return but there is no reason to believe this is true especially in the new/new quadrant. When companies use the Ansoff matrix in this way without any additional intervention (such as a capabilities approach), they are likely skewing their strategy to higher risk initiatives which will likely yield lower not higher returns.

Finding Your Sweet Spots!

As we alluded to above, our suggested approach is actually embedded in Ansoff's original article. We believe the first step is to define the company's differentiating capabilities, what we are really good at. Then develop a set of potential growth opportunities where we believe those capabilities may solve problems for a set of customers, we call these our sweet spots.

In Grassroots Strategy we describe finding your Strategic Sweet-spots, or "natural right to win" opportunities. Those sweet-spots are intersections of what you are uniquely qualified to provide with customer needs in the market.

Once you have generated this list of potential sweet spots, develop and evaluate each of these sweet spots using basic strategic marketing principles, what we call our Grassroot Strategy Framework.

Specifically make sure that you:

- Define both current and available markets in terms of the problems you solve for the customer.

- Understand the economic value of solving these problems in better or different ways.

- Segment the market based on differences in customers' needs.

- Develop segment-specific value propositions that leverage your differentiation (either current or potential)

With this market-back perspective, you're ready to develop a more informed assessment of growth opportunities. You will identify winning business opportunities and follow them where they go, not just try to

populate the matrix. Diversification may be one of the outcomes of this market-back approach, whereas pursuing diversification for its own sake almost always leads you astray.

As Ansoff points out, there can be inherent risk in doing ONLY current market/product penetration, because eventually markets evolve – IBM would no longer exist if they had remained a mainframe computer company. But part of the reason that a market-back perspective is so critical is that the cost and risk of trying to grow in the other quadrants is non-linear – it grows exponentially as you move farther from customers and products you know well. Specifically, we believe:

- Taking new products to existing customers is often incrementally riskier than your home quadrant, but often not dramatically so. Especially if you differentiate not just with product features, finding ways to add more value for customers you know well (and know you) is usually not a big stretch.

- The risk of taking existing products to new markets is often overlooked.

The key to mitigating this risk is building the detailed market understanding of customer needs and their current alternatives (not assuming they are the same as the customers you know well), then proceeding only where there is a clear under-met need that your differentiated capabilities can plausibly fill. Details matter here – For example, we have seen an aerospace company fail in the automotive market because they assumed that a technically less complicated product meant a less demanding customer, when in fact, the opposite turned out to be true.

- The last quadrant, pure diversification, is almost always a bad idea – the costs and risks are clearly the highest but there is no reason to expect higher returns. Here we begin to step into the realm that Donald Rumsfeld famously referred to as the unknown-unknowns. Ansoff calls these 'unknowable risks,' and we would agree.

The key is not better defining your aspirations, but rather a grounded and objective market-back perspective on your differentiating capabilities and how they might add value with products and customers that you don't know. A thorough market study of customers, competitors and current offerings is necessary to reduce this risk, but realistically will not eliminate it.

In the end, while we might quibble with Ansoff's detailed approach, we strongly agree with his original premise: evolving with markets is key, but diversification of any kind without a clear view the capabilities that will allow you to win is a recipe for disaster.

Summary

The Ansoff matrix can be a great tool for ensuring coverage of the range of opportunities to be explored in a growth strategy. But what should be clear is that the ultimate growth strategy should be grounded in market economics and differentiation. While mechanisms of achieving growth vary significantly across the quadrants, the growth journey always starts with an outside in view of your differentiation – being ruthlessly objective is the only way to make this work.

We are reminded on an old saying: "don't marry for money… only date rich people and then marry for love." Translating this for our clients, we might say "don't chase growth for its own sake…only look where you can provide value through your differentiation and the growth will follow."

Product Management Holds the Keys to Effective Strategic Marketing

May 31, 2024

Over the years we have written several articles about the pitfalls of focusing too much on your product, including: Is it time to take the 'product' out of product management? and Warning: No-one Cares About Your Product! This time we are going to make the case that product management is about more than just your physical product and when done right it is actually the essence of good strategic marketing. Not only that, but product management should be a core focus of general management because it encompasses the majority of what it takes to be a successful general manager.

Small "p" Product Management

It is easy to get trapped in a tautological definition of product management – "the product manager manages the product." This product-first thinking means that critical elements of value and delivery are left to other parts of the organization. Marketing decides what the message should be, sales decides what they should sell to which customers, customer service decides which customers are most important and how to serve them, etc. This leaves the business with no more than a hope that everyone's objectives are aligned around a winning strategy.

An example of what can happen when companies are too focused on the product aspect of product management was the thermostat market up through 2010. The electric thermostat is not a new product by any means. It was invented by Warren Johnson in 1883 and launched when he founded Johnson Controls in 1885.

The only meaningful innovation in the category for the next 120 years was the programmable thermostat, allowing customers to "manage the tradeoff between comfort and energy usage" by having different temperature setpoints by time of day. By the early 2000's, analog thermostats were now digital, and the majority of new thermostats installed could be programmed. Yet the US Energy

Information Agency estimated that only 19 percent of these thermostats were programmed. This means that over 80% of those programmable thermostats were set on permanent "hold" – probably adjusted only twice per year to switch from heat to cool and vice versa. Thus, for most of the market the programmable thermostat delivered no more value than the original basic electric thermostat developed by Professor Johnson in 1883.

In 2011 Tony Fadell, the "father of the iPod," launched The Nest Learning Thermostat and turned the thermostat market on its head. Like he had done with the iPod, he recognized that there was a significant part of the market that was being underserved by the programmable thermostats of the day. Those thermostats had been designed by engineers for engineers and while some would argue they are technically superior to the Nest; they were not being used to their fullest. The problem was that they were too complex for the typical homeowner.

The entire thermostat market had been focused on the best technical product to solve the problem, rather than the best and easiest solution to solve the bigger problem for the customer. Fadell, clearly channeling his success with the iPod, realized that solving the customer problem ('a programable thermostat that you don't need to program), required a different value proposition, a different channel and ultimately a different business model, NOT just a better 'product.'

The Way Out – Expand the Role of Product Management

As this example highlights, the role of Product Management is all too often limited to managing the product specification, and this can lead to disaster. In our view, Product Management should not be primarily about the current product, rather it should be the champion of your entire strategic marketing process. In our Grassroots Strategy workshops and book we walk through a strategic marketing framework to improve the commercial success of your business. This is precisely the mission of good product management, and thus exactly the relevant toolkit.

The core responsibility of product management is to ensure that your entire offering meets market needs and creates significant customer value. In addition, you must have a business model that captures that value. When done properly, the product management orchestrates the interface between the

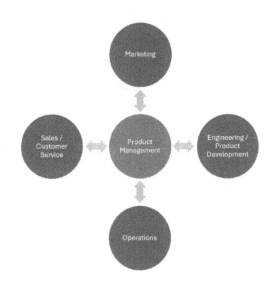

market (customers) and your entire organization. It requires deep interaction with the entire organization, including sales, marketing, customer service, operations, and engineering. The product manager must harmonize these functions to achieve a common goal: delivering value to customers while aligning with the business's strategic objectives.

Bridging Sales and Customer Insights

One of the primary responsibilities of a Product Manager is to serve as a bridge between the organization and the people interacting with customers on a regular basis, aka sales and customer service. Ideally, the Product Manager should gather crucial customer needs and feedback through direct interaction with customers. In addition, they should also gather customer needs and feedback through the commercial teams, since they are on the frontline, interacting directly with customers on a daily basis. In return, product managers should equip the sales team with robust value propositions and value pricing strategies, enabling them to effectively communicate the product's benefits and justify its value, thereby enhancing customer acquisition, retention and profitability.

Collaborating with Engineering and Development

The collaboration between Product Managers and the engineering or product development teams is vital for innovation. Product Managers must understand what is technically feasible and economically viable in these teams. They also should create and refine the product roadmap based on segmentation and customer value, which outlines the future direction and enhancements of the product. This roadmap is essential for keeping the development efforts aligned with market needs and technological advancements.

Synthesizing Go-To-Market Plans

Product Managers should also work closely with the marketing department to refine and target the go-to-market plans. By providing insights on market trends and customer needs, they help marketing tailor messages that resonate with the target customer segments. They should define clear value propositions that the marketing team can use to attract potential customers. This ensures that the go-to-market plans are targeted by customer segment and messaging is compelling because it focuses on solving customer problems and delivering economic value.

Aligning with Operations

A critical yet often overlooked aspect of product management is the alignment with operations. Product Managers should perform the trade-off analysis between customer needs, engineering specifications, and manufacturability to achieve a cost that aligns with (ideally is well below) the customer value delivered. Product management should also be involved in forecasting and understand the impact of accurate forecasts up and down the P&L.

Product Management as a Training Ground for General Managers

The skills homed in Product Management—strategic thinking, cross-functional leadership, market insight, customer focus, and operational coordination—are also the hallmarks of a great general manager. Product Managers are uniquely positioned to understand the business from a holistic perspective, making them prime candidates for general management roles.

By managing a product across its lifecycle, they learn to balance short-term successes with long-term goals, manage diverse teams, and make decisions that affect the entire business. This comprehensive experience prepares them to become effective leaders who can navigate complex business environments and prepares them for larger roles.

Conclusion

A skilled Product Manager orchestrates the interface between the market and your entire organization, and our Grassroots Strategy framework is exactly the toolkit they need to successfully drive this interaction. As they coordinate various functions within the organization, Product Managers should drive them towards a unified objective of delivering and capturing exceptional customer value. As businesses continue to navigate increasingly competitive markets, the role of the Product Manager will become ever more crucial, not just in managing products but in leading businesses towards sustainable growth and profitability.

Section 2: Market and Customer Understanding

Introduction

Some of our clients call the Grassroots Strategy approach "market-back strategy" because it starts with a firm understanding of both your customers and the entire market. Far too many B2B companies start with the product and just hope that there is a market for their offering. This may work sometimes, but a strategy that is grounded in market realities aimed at solving real customer problems is much more likely to be successful.

The first step is realizing that no-one really wants to buy your product. They want the positive business outcomes that your offering hopefully helps them to achieve. That requires a deep understanding of your customer's business and the problems (both solved and unsolved) you can help them with.

And, unfortunately you and your customers don't exist in a vacuum. You both exist in an overall market ecosystem that often includes many other players in the value chain. A thorough understanding of the entire market economics can help to identify gaps and/or opportunities to unlock end-customer value.

These stories touch on various aspects of value chain economics, customer needs, and how to unlock value with your product roadmap. Hopefully you find them interesting and that they provide useful tools that you can apply to better understand your markets and customers.

Warning: No-one Cares About Your Product!

October 3, 2020

Our executive sponsor at a long-time client used to start off every Grassroots Strategy session by telling the teams to put a jar in the middle of their table and every time someone mentioned the word 'product' they had to put $5 in it. She told them that she was sure that every team would be able to throw a pretty good party by the end of the week with the money they collected. Her point was that they needed to focus on the customer and the problems that they could solve for customers rather than on their product. Professor Theodore Levitt said it best decades ago when he said, "People don't want to buy a quarter-inch drill. They want a quarter-inch hole."

To a certain extent, the focus on products is understandable. We organize marketing around 'product managers,' we report revenue and profit by product line and we even report on the progress of innovation as 'new product development.' But good marketers understand that they must break this cycle of internal thinking – it is not what we want those matters, rather it is the customer who decides whether our product makes them better off. The success of our product line or new product launches is the result, not the cause.

Start with the Problems You Solve for Customers

The first step in understanding your market is to really evaluate what problem or problems you solve for your customer. What is the "hole" that you provide in Dr. Levitt's analogy? Try to step back and think about what job.

your customer is hiring your company to do on their behalf with your offering? If you didn't have a product and you were applying to your customer for a job, what would the job description say? (Clayton Christensen, et al. HBR, September 2016) This is often a surprisingly difficult thing for people to do. But it is amazing what you will find when you stop thinking that you are in the business of selling drill bits and get into the mode of thinking that you help people make holes. Sometimes this even requires you to step back even further and think about who your customer really is. Who are you solving the problem for? Is it a distributor, an installer, a consumer, or maybe even an end-user who is not involved in the buying decision? Done well, this simple shift in perspective can change the entire way you think about your business.

An Example

A very powerful example of thinking customer problem back rather than product forward is Apple's launch of the iPod in 2000. If they were thinking product forward, they would have tried to introduce the best MP3 player on the market. It turns out that from a product perspective what they actually launched was a device that leveraged mostly 3-year-old technology. The half-life of technology in consumer electronics is measured in months, not years, so from a technical standpoint their product was in the dark ages. How did they win? By recognizing that they were trying to get into the "mobile music" market. By coming at it from that perspective, they were able to realize that there were two limiting factors to adoption of MP3 players: ease of use and legality. They were able to address the two fundamental reasons that more people weren't buying MP3 players by making it easier to use and legal through the iTunes eco-system as an alternative to Napster. Apple's success had very little to do with the device (product) and everything to do with the limitations on the existing solutions to be able to solve that primary customer problem (mobile music).

Consider the Customer's Alternatives

Another advantage of thinking about the problem you are solving from the customer's perspective is that it allows you to consider all of the alternative ways to solve the problem. In the hole example, depending on the size and precisions of the hole, you could use a hammer and chisel, hire a contractor, use a CNC machine, or today build around the hole with 3D printing, in essence making a part with the hole already in it.

In the MP3 player example, the best alternative for most people was a Walkman, Discman, or portable radio. It wasn't a competing MP3 player, because most people either couldn't or weren't willing to use them. If you can truly get to the place where you understand the problem the customer is trying to solve, then you can evaluate all ways the customer could solve that problem. These examples also highlight that there are benefits to this way of thinking both for offense and defense – these alternative solutions could either be threats to your current product or opportunities to dramatically expand your customer base.

Expand Your Thinking

Also, by thinking from the customer's perspective you can start to think about what else you could do to help the customer solve the problem. Are there other services or ways of helping them that will provide a better solution to the problem? Remember, Apple was a failing computer company in 2000. They were not a consumer electronics company nor were they a content provider. But by solving a customer problem, they were able to transform not just the MP3 market, but the entire music industry. And as iTunes has evolved into the App store, they have created an entirely new business model that is not dependent on a hardware sale.

Conclusion

One of the fundamental things to understand is that customers don't buy your product because they want your product, they buy it because of the problem that it solves for them. In fact, in B2B, if your customers could make more money by buying nothing at all that would be preferable. Occasionally, they may buy from you because they like you, which is nice, but rarely sustainable in a B2B setting. B2B customers buy things that help them solve problems – i.e., they do a job that makes their business more money. So, stop thinking that the world revolves around your product. Instead, invest in understanding how you can help your customers improve their business first, and great product ideas will follow!

Value Chain Economics: The Secret to Market Leadership

March 9, 2022

One of the first things we have our clients do in our Grassroots Strategy workshops is define the market or "opportunity" from their customer's perspective. The primary question we ask is "what is the problem you solve for the customer?" Seems simple, right? Not always. Answering that question is predicated on understanding who is the customer that you solve a problem for. It is far too easy, and comfortable, to just focus on your direct customer, the company that buys from you, but is that really where you create differential value?

Often the customer where you really solve a problem is two, three or even more steps down the value chain. As we like to say, "if there is a better way to solve the end customer's problem, someone will find it. Don't you want that someone to be you?" Said differently, you can do the best job in the world of serving a wholesale channel, but if end-customers start buying online bypassing the wholesaler, you will be out of business. In B-to-B markets, your customer is almost always part of a bigger eco-system. Understanding the economics of all the players in that eco-system is critical to identifying new opportunities.

Several client examples come to mind. The first example is a company that had developed an additive for asphalt that made the asphalt more stable. Asphalt companies were interested in the new additive but were not willing to pay a significant amount more than existing additives that didn't perform as well. The asphalt companies argued that a higher priced additive would increase their costs enough to make their asphalt uncompetitive in what was a highly price competitive market. When the company began speaking directly with road construction companies and road owners, they realized that the potential value of their additive was significant; either through the reduction in the amount of asphalt required for a given road and/or in making roads (particularly in high stress environments) last longer.

The company came to the conclusion that in order to get the value out of their new product they would need to market their product to their customers' customers. The company hired several engineers from the road construction industry and began to market directly to road owners. Eventually they were able to drive specifications in road construction projects to be favorable to the use of their new product and developed a market for their new additive at a significantly higher price-point than other performance additives. Obviously, selling efforts down the value chain can be costly and time-consuming, but if we only focus on our direct customers, we may never understand the true value we create. In this case, it was enough value to justify a change in business model.

A second example is a company that made tackifier. For those not in the adhesives industry, a tackifier is the material that makes glue sticky before it cures. It is a very important component in an adhesive; so much so that it constitutes about a third of the cost of making an adhesive. Our client had developed a better performing tackifier and wanted to get paid for the value of its better performance. Not surprisingly, when our client talked to their direct customer, the adhesive maker, they wanted one of two things: lower their price or allow them to use less of the material.

It quickly became clear that in order to get paid for the value of the better performing tackifier, they would have to solve a problem for their customer's customer. The original intended target was food packaging applications, specifically "hot-melt" adhesives on cereal boxes. However, it turns out that current adhesives largely met the needs of food packaging companies, and the risk of switching was so high that it wasn't worth even evaluating new alternatives, because the lost productivity during the evaluation would swamp any potential benefits. And it turns out that the cost of all of the adhesive going into a box of cereal is less than $0.01, so the cost of the tackifier was less than 1/3 of $0.01 per box. Even if they lowered the tackifier price to zero, it is unlikely that the cereal maker would consider changing suppliers. Although not the answer they were hoping for, they were able to refocus their efforts on other applications where a better performing tackifier would actually solve a problem for an end-customer.

Another client was a very successful supplier of hardware for residential security systems. They had a broad product line and excellent product availability which made them the easy choice for distributors. They focused their "marketing" efforts on distributors, strengthening their relationships with rebate programs and reward trips. When we tried to get them to think about value further down the value chain, they were reluctant to even consider it. For example, when we pointed out that their own research showed that nearly 50 percent of home security systems were turned off because of experience with false alarms (a great example of an unsolved customer problem!), their response was essentially "not my problem".

Eventually their business began to decline and so the company started to look into the economics of the value chain. They learned that while they made very high percentage profit, measured in dollars, distributors, installers and monitoring companies all made significantly more than they did. Moreover, the monitoring companies had recurring revenue meaning that our client was extracting no more than about five percent of the lifetime value of the system that their hardware enabled. More importantly, it turns out that there IS a better way to solve the end- customer problem – DIY systems such as SimpliSafe were allowing consumers to install components themselves and monitor the system on their smartphones, bypassing the installer and reducing monitoring fees dramatically.

Because our client had been focused on distributors, they had been missing the opportunity to capture more value and were now seeing their core business in decline. Developing an understanding of their customer's customer and the economics down the value chain allowed our client to begin rethinking their approach to the market and begin to take corrective action to preserve their core market and expand into adjacent areas.

There are several things that you can learn by analyzing the economics of your value chain. Here are some specific things to look for:

1. How big is the total value chain, not just the direct market for your products?

2. How important is your part of the value chain to the customer? From the customers' perspective, are you their mortgage payment or their dry-cleaning bill?

3. What are the steps between you and the end-customer and how do they create value? Are there opportunities to forward integrate to capture more of the total solution?

4. Who makes money throughout the value chain, and why? Are there things that you can do to create more value or capture more of the value created?

5. Are there ways that technology could (or is already) impact the established value chain (for example, could on-line tools dramatically reduce search costs and change the role of personal relationships)?

As you think through these questions, the key is to distance yourself from current products and practices and keep asking, "is there a better way to serve the end customer?" As we've said, if there is a better way, someone will find it. In fact, in today's world with technology start-ups and new business models, the reality may be that someone else already has found it.

Bottom line, evaluating every level of your value chain, from you to the very end customer, can help you to understand the total potential value of your offering. and identify opportunities to capture that value. It can help you to think about where you actually create value and break out of the myopic focus on your direct customer. It may provide an early warning system for big value shifts in your industry and/or highlight opportunities to repackage your capabilities and create even more value for your customers.

Taking the Customer's Perspective?

April 5, 2022

OK, time for a quick test. If you were looking at this menu board, what would you expect to pay for a bottle of Piper Heidsick champagne? [photo showed a chalkboard menu that under 'by the bottle,' had $33 somewhat aligned with the words 'Piper Heidsick.']

This is a real picture of the menu board that my wife and I were faced with on a recent Friday evening (I have doctored it only to compensate for my poor photography skills). We decided to order a bottle of champagne to celebrate – maybe just celebrating the fact that it was Friday. By our read of this menu, the Heidsick was a great deal at just $33 per bottle. We were somewhat surprised when we got the bill, and the bottle was priced at $65!

I said surprised, not shocked – I know this bottle is around $45 in our local wine shop, so $65 is a reasonable restaurant price, and $33 did seem like a steal. Nonetheless, I pointed it out to the restaurant. After paying our bill, I said to the owner "This is not a complaint, I know that $65 is about the market price for that bottle of champagne, and we probably would have ordered it anyway. But a reasonable person could look at your chalkboard and expect to pay $33, you might want to change that." To my dismay, the response was basically a silent stare, and inexplicably when we went back to the restaurant two weeks later, the sign was unchanged!

Thinking about how this could happen, I realized that this is a problem for many of our clients as well – the difficulty of taking the customer's perspective. In this case, the restauranteur knew (because she had done it) that the $33 referred to another bottle that they had erased when they ran out of it, and it wasn't important that the champagne did not have a price because it was rarely ordered anyway and their cost fluctuated based on the availability to their supplier. She expected that anyone ordering champagne would either ask about the price, or didn't care about the price. From the perspective of the person who runs the restaurant it was no big deal. Unfortunately, as a patron seeing the chalkboard for the first time, it is easy to reach a different conclusion, and it matters.

When we talk to our clients about VOC, framing issues from the customer's perspective is critical to understanding potential problems we could solve and the value they would place on solving them, but it is often difficult to get past our perspective. We have talked before about our client who makes garage door openers. Understandably, they think about garage door openers 45-plus hours per week and know model numbers, horsepower ratings, decibel levels and competitor strengths and weaknesses.

Contrast this with what they know about how homeowners think – you and I generally don't think about our garage door opener at all until it breaks (which is only about once every 12 – 15 years) and then most of us are in the market for about one hour – we are not doing exhaustive research and weighing technical trade-offs, rather we are seeing who can get to our house most quickly and almost always buying what that technician happens to have on the truck. Any winning stratagem must work in this reality, not just be attractive to garage door opener experts.

So how do you avoid the trap of projecting your knowledge and biases onto your customers and focusing on what matters to you and not what matters to them? We've come up with four practical tips to help you keep the right perspective:

1. Go out of your way to adopt your customer's *point of view*. In this case, come out from behind the bar and look at the chalkboard as if it were the first time you were seeing it. For many of our clients this might mean leaving the comfort of your desk (or home office) and going out to the field – try reading the instructions and installing your product in a dark utility room in the basement of a half-finished building as opposed to doing it on your well-lit lab bench.

2. Make sure you understand your customer's **process** – observe the customer along their entire journey, from identifying the need to buying something to maintaining the product, or maybe even disposing of it at

the end of its life. Where are their pain points and how might we address them through better search, documentation, support or maybe just better packaging?

3. Develop an appreciation of your customer's *priorities* – what are they trying to accomplish as a business and how does your offering fit in? Are you a large piece of their cost structure or a small piece? Does handling your offering consume a lot of their mental energy or is their business focused elsewhere? We have said it before, knowing what WE want is the easy part (buy more from us at higher prices), but facing the fact that the customer would prefer to buy less at lower prices, or maybe not buy from us at all can be difficult.

4. Lastly, and perhaps most importantly, understand how your customers make a *profit*. Like much of what we talk about, one of the central elements of good B2B marketing is an objective view of customer value. How important is the problem you solve for them? What is your differential value in solving that problem relative to their switching cost? It is not enough to list all the attributes or even benefits that we think a customer would like, our goal is to understand how they make trade-offs. A customer may, in fact, want lighter weight, smaller size, longer battery life and lower cost – but if they can't have all four at once, how do they decide? If we can't answer that, our job is not finished.

As should be clear, doing this right requires interacting with customers beyond a typical sales call to gain insight into how they think and why they make the choices they make. This may not be a habit, and it may even seem uncomfortable at first, but there is no substitute for direct observation.

In one dramatic example of this, we worked with a company that made components for building control systems. They identified that they had been losing share in multi-story office buildings and couldn't understand why. When their engineers tested the competitors' products alongside their own – component by component our client's were more robust, easier to use and about the same price. So, what was behind the share loss?

When they visited a job site, the answer was almost instantly clear. Our client packaged their products in a way that made sense in their factory – all the thermostats in one box, all the smoke detectors in another box, etc. What this meant was that when contractors were ready to install the controls on one floor of the building, they needed to open all the boxes to pull the necessary products. The remaining parts were left in open boxes which needed to be pulled together again when the next floor was ready, assuming no parts had 'disappeared' from the open boxes laying around the job site.

In contrast, their competitor took the time to package products by floor – one box containing all the devices needed for a single floor of the building was delivered as needed. Armed with this understanding, our client was able to copy the competitor's practice and stem the market share loss. Over time, they did even better, finding opportunities to prewire components saving on-site labor and automating calibration steps using smart-phone based tools – none of which would have been on their product roadmap had they not committed to direct observation.

Taking the customer's perspective may require stepping out of your comfort zone and you may not always like what you see. But there is no better way to understand your customers' context and decision-making process and how you can impact it.

Oh, the restaurant... we may go back eventually (you'll notice I did not mention their name). The food is very good, and the service is otherwise excellent, but I have to admit the complete inability to see things from my perspective leaves a sour taste in my mouth (despite the delicious champagne) – not how you want your customers to feel, regardless of your business.

Don't Apply the B2C Customer Journey to B2B

August 25, 2022

Regular readers of our blog know that we have an instinctive negative reaction to consumer marketing concepts being applied in B2B. Ideas like personas and brand equity are critical in B2C marketing, but when inappropriately applied in B2B they can drive bad decisions based on customer preferences and personalities as opposed to real business needs and the economics underlying those needs. So, it would not surprise you that we were initially skeptical about applying the concept of "customer journey" to B2B markets.

In researching the topic, we found no shortage of customer mapping tools and templates available on-line. However, unlike some earlier business fads, there does not seem to be one generally accepted method for documenting a customer journey. We found many websites that offered their journey template and others that said it can't be reduced to a template. We even found one website that offered this sage advice to the novice: "Customer journey mapping is the process of creating a customer journey map". In addition, much of the material is built for the digital customer experience. This is understandable, as understanding why and where potential customers are abandoning carts, for example, is critical in digital B2C channels. The literature is less helpful in how to apply to hybrid or personal touch channels still found in much of the B2B world. Against the noise, however, there does seem to be agreement that the basic steps of a customer journey are: awareness, consideration, conversion, loyalty and advocacy. Needless to say, this list describes a *consumer* journey and does not fit the reality of most B2B purchasing behavior.

Imagine for example that your company makes composite parts for the aerospace industry. You may want to map a customer journey for, say, Boeing. Does their journey start with awareness? Most likely you have done business with them for years. Consideration and conversion may be your goals, but we would argue that getting to the underlying needs of the business is the way to achieve them. And lastly, loyalty and advocacy have even less relevance – a purchasing manager at Boeing would get fired for buying based on loyalty if it is not the best economic outcome for the company, and they would get fired even faster if they encouraged a competitor to use the same supplier!

Suppressing our initial instinct to reject the concept completely, we dug a little deeper and realized that beneath the hype, there are some critical ideas around customer journey that are absolutely applicable in B2B.

A recent client example helped us crystallize the relevant pieces. Our client had a division that distributed specialized 'furniture' used in scientific laboratories (lab benches, shelves cabinets, etc.). The business was reasonably profitable but was barely growing at the rate of GDP. They sold single items for replacement or lab expansion but realized that their big-ticket sales were usually associated with the construction of a new lab.

When we began to talk about customer value and potential differentiation around this purchase occasion, we quickly hit a dead-end. After some back and forth, the team realized that they only saw a fraction of the customer journey, specifically the part that started with them receiving a request for a quote on a given list of furniture. Knowing that this was insufficient, the team set out to do some broader VOC to understand the complete decision process.

What they discovered was a lengthy process of lab design and budget approvals. Then customers, or the designers and consultants they hired, selected suppliers for each category of equipment, including furniture. Once the equipment started to arrive, the customer (or their contractor) needed to find people qualified to install it, connect it and debug it. They then needed to stock the lab with consumables and hire and train people to work there.

In short, they discovered an entire universe of parties involved in the decision and installation process, many of whom they had not spoken with before. When they started to do VOC up and down this value chain they discovered dozens of pain-points that they could address by getting more involved in the design phase. For example, using knowledge of lab workflows they could leverage 3D modeling capabilities to optimize layouts and even customize furniture to ensure that all the items being ordered would fit properly and work better (e.g., making sure a lab bench will be the same length as the vent hood that needs to go above it). By re-thinking their business and then adapting their go to market approach, this once overlooked division is now on a steep growth trajectory.

Mapping this B2B customer journey alongside our client reinforced four key themes:

1. Make sure you understand the eco-system in which your offering exists. Is your offering ultimately used as part of a bigger package? Is the bigger package designed around your offering or does your offering need to conform to the design of the bigger package? Who specifies the bigger package? Who specifies the requirements for your offering within the bigger package? Who integrates/installs your offering? Who maintains it?

2. Invest in documenting the entire customer journey, end-to-end. This should include the journey pre-sale, and post-sale. For example, how do they gather information? What design decisions need to be made? How do they make those decisions? What are the issues with how they install your offering, use it, upgrade and potentially even dispose of it?

3. Keep your eyes open for pain-points. In our story above, one of the clients was visiting a major university with multiple labs on the campus. On the day of her visit, one of the contractors was cursing that he was going to have to return a lab table that would not fit through the door to the lab. Trained in good VOC principles, our client asked how often this happens. The contractor shook his head, "almost every job. It's as if the people designing the lab don't talk to each other." The idea of using 3D software was born.

4. You may be able to reimagine customer engagement by capturing a broader set of "touchpoints". – In the case above, enabling designers to deliver a faster timeline and less returned product for a new lab would give them a reason to use your software and specify your product.

The focus of B2B businesses should be to create economic value for their customers. Effective B2B marketing requires articulating economic value in the form of a clear value proposition. Understanding the full "customer journey" for the B2B customer helps to identify value you may have otherwise missed. Equally important, make sure you tailor and communicate the value proposition to the influencers and actual decision maker that ultimately impact the purchase of your offering.

Unlocking the Value Chain

May 19, 2023

When we conduct our Grassroots Strategy workshops, a task on day one is to draw your value chain – the steps your offering goes through before reaching an end-user. In the business-to-business world, value chains can include different distributors, specifiers, installers and value-added resellers, all of whom can influence what gets bought by whom. We recommend looking at not just product flow, but also at how decisions and money flow up and down this chain.

Getting this structure on paper is a foundational step in understanding your market. One recent example stands out, where really understanding the value chain and the economics of the players held the key to a winning strategy.

This particular client made components for on-highway trucks. The product line we were focused on could be sold in several ways – as standard equipment on a new vehicle, as part of a "user-specified" configuration or installed as an aftermarket replacement at a truck dealer. The ultimate end-user was either a fleet or an individual owner- operator, but the entire chain was involved in the decision:

We realized that the chart was equivalent to a logic diagram with 'gates' that had to line up. For example, if sales could not convince the OE to include the product line as standard equipment, they would need to convince both OEMs and country level managers to include the product line as an authorized user configuration. But at that point, while owners could be persuaded to ask for our client's product, if the dealer found it too difficult to configure (or if configuration caused delays), the dealer would usually talk him out of it.

As we talked through the market, it also became clear that the decision process and roles were quite different by OEM. At the time there were seven primary truck OEMs operating in Europe. Some drove all key decisions centrally, offering little or no opportunity for customization. Others were much more flexible, giving the country- level managers and dealers more autonomy for custom configurations and aftermarket replacement options.

Combined, these insights were critical in helping prioritize where to spend sales time. Previous efforts had been mostly around trying to influence end-users and their perception of value (ease of use, safety, lifecycle cost). But armed with this broader perspective, it was clear that some of these efforts were wasted – for example, preference would be irrelevant for a user who was locked into one of the inflexible OEMs (in the extreme, changing one component might even void the vehicle level warranty).

In addition, this insight helped surface new opportunities, like training dealers to use the configuration software and so removing a potential decision blocker. Using this insight to prioritize sales efforts turned out to be particularly critical for this client, whose salesforce was typically exactly one person per major country in Europe! Needless to say, they couldn't afford to waste a lot of time calling on customers who would never generate an incremental sale.

As a general rule, you should periodically revisit the value chain for your offerings. Some things to look out for:

- Do different competitors and/or potential customers have different value chains?

- Are there channels that are gaining share at the expense of others (like e-commerce) and why are customers shifting?

- Are there alternative ways to create value for end-users that might bypass traditional channels?

- Are the economics of key decision makers changing in terms of search cost, switching costs, etc.?

- Are there influencers or potential blockers that may limit our ability to impact end-user decisions?

- Ultimately, are we spending our scarce sales time at the most important leverage points in this chain?

In summary the value chain exercise is a critical piece of the overall Grassroots Strategy logic and cannot be skipped. More importantly, thorough documentation of not just product flow, but decision and money flow throughout the chain can provide key insights into the economics of the decision makers and influencers. On occasion, this can fundamentally change how we approach a market or even change our view of 'who is the customer?'

Thinking like your Customers' Buyers

June 20, 2023

(How to use your customers' strategic sourcing framework to find your sweet spots.)

We recently completed an adjacent-market strategy project for an automotive supplier looking to diversify beyond the cyclical and price-sensitive auto OEMS into adjacent markets with similar technology needs. For them, like many of us, the phrase "strategic sourcing" conjured up images of scowling purchasing managers at their automotive customers devising ever more diabolic approaches to drive down their prices.

At first glance, other markets seemed more attractive – while they were somewhat lower volume than automotive, they did not have the reputation of cutthroat automotive purchasing departments and might make it easier for our client to get a good return on their application engineering investment. Our job was to help them figure out where to focus, separating the 'grass is greener' bias from the reality of how these adjacent market customers make buying decisions.

It is generally true that purchasing managers focus on driving down prices – they don't design the part or determine the number of pieces, so getting the best price is how they add value. However, even companies with the worst reputations for aggressive price negotiation have adopted some form of strategic sourcing framework. They have acknowledged that just driving down cost per part is not enough if you don't have access to the supplier's best technology, or worse drive the supplier out of business (again, see automotive).

As a result, most companies work with established frameworks for categorizing purchases and developing appropriate sourcing strategies for different categories that explicitly acknowledge the value a supplier can bring beyond simply lowering price. Better understanding how your customers apply these strategic sourcing frameworks can help inform suppliers as to how to best target and approach markets, segment them and develop specific value propositions to bring to customers.

How does strategic sourcing approach the supply market?

One well established framework for strategic sourcing is referred to as Kraljic's matrix (1). The matrix characterizes purchase categories based on two dimensions: business importance and market risk / complexity. Business importance refers to the category's influence on profitability but is often simply gauged based on the proportion of cost represented. Supply Risk/Complexity refers to the ability to secure supply at competitive costs; this is typically driven by the degree of competition, pace of technology evolution, complexity of logistics, and so on.

The following table, adapted from Kraljic's article, summarizes the framework.

As a business, you'll end up with spending in all four quadrants. You'll also do everything possible to drive suppliers to the lower left or at least convince them that that is where they are in an effort to get better prices. But the reality is that you will still end up with suppliers in all four quadrants.

How can we turn strategic sourcing around and apply it to suppliers?

As a supplier, with each market or market segment that you approach, you will end up in different quadrants from the customers' perspective. For your business, the priority markets will be those for which you are positioned to the right side and preferably lower right (everything else equal) of the matrix. You may not be able to ignore the markets/segments on the left if that is where the volume is (again, see: automotive), but if that is all you do, you are defining competition as a race to commoditization.

So, from a strategic growth perspective, your energy should be focused on the evolving features and capabilities that will help drive you to, or better yet, grow your business on the right-hand side of the matrix.

The first step in applying this framework as a supplier is to understand where purchasing teams in each market (and eventually each market segment) see your business in the matrix.

To gauge importance to the customers' business (the vertical axis), a great starting point can be your price as a proportion of the customer's cost. There is a

Your Perspective on Customers

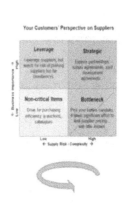

100

bit of judgment in gauging this, but if you are getting the attention of customer category managers on a regular basis vs working through buyers, you're of higher importance.

To gauge Supply Risk / Complexity for the customer (the horizontal axis), a simple proxy is assessing how many supply options a customer could secure in relatively short order. If there are multiple options, you're on the left side; if there are few, you're on the right side. Beyond that first pass, you will also want to consider specific differentiation of your own offering: intellectual property or process know-how, product and service differentiation, level of knowledge of and integration with customer's process, etc.

What are the implications on strategy and execution for suppliers?

Strategy starts with an understanding of where you are in the matrix with existing customers, but that is just the baseline. Your goal should be to focus on products/services that create differential value and can (even temporarily) move you to the more attractive righthand side.

When evaluating new business opportunities (organic), the key is to assess where your offering would land in the matrix above for the new markets (and segments) being considered. To properly gauge the horizontal axis, you will need to understand what problems we solve for the customer, what value we add vs the next best alternative and whether there are few or many alternatives that can solve the same problem. Building this understanding before entering a market, either organically or through acquisition, will help you avoid the trap of starting with a 'me-too' offering that only accelerates commoditization.

How did this apply to our automotive supplier client?

Our automotive client recognized that despite the reputation of automotive customers, much of their automotive business was towards the upper right-hand corner of Kraljic's matrix. However, to ensure the ongoing profitability of their existing automotive business, they were in a constant battle to innovate and maintain their position on the right-hand side of the matrix.

When applying this thinking to new business opportunities, the client was able to better recognize that in several vertical markets the major customer had deep engineering expertise, and so potential customers would quickly take the integration of our client's offering in-house and so shift our client to a more commodity-like purchase to the left of Kradjic's matrix. On the other hand, in several other vertical markets where the clients' offering was of similar business importance the potential customers didn't have the scale to vertically integrate; here the client was a strong candidate for a strategic partner.

Despite a better understanding of Kradjic's matrix our client still thinks of "strategic sourcing" as scowling purchasing managers devising diabolical schemes to drive down prices and ruin their profitability. However, with this more informed perspective, the client was better able focus on the best target markets and segments where players were facing specific technical challenges and needed to rely on supply partnerships. The analysis provided additional insights that guided specific focus within each segment on the aspects of the client's offering that were "strategic" or "leverage" opportunities in those markets / segments.

Wrapping up

Turning the sourcing strategy around allows you to think like your customers. It can provide a critical perspective on how and where you can best add value, informing how to best target and approach markets, segments and individual organizations for selling. This is useful in guiding strategy and execution in both your home markets and when considering adjacent markets.

[1] Kraljic, Peter (September 1983). *"Purchasing Must Become Supply Management"*. (https://hbr.org/1983/09/purchasing-must-become-supply-management) Harvard Business Review.

Drive Growth Using Customer Value to Shape Your Product Roadmap

November 2, 2023

I was very intrigued when our client declared they would also be using their value selling tool to evaluate and prioritize their product development roadmap. Although we specifically designed the tool for marketing and sales, the more I thought about it, the more this strategy made sense.

We constantly preach that you should sell based on the value you create, but if your product development isn't continuously focused on creating more value, your success will diminish over time.

Using Customer Value to Prioritize Your Roadmap

The goal of your product roadmap should be to continuously improve your offering in ways that attract new customers and encourage existing customers to continue using your offering. The best way to do this is to continually find ways to create more business value.

In two recent blog posts, *Five Requirements to Being a Value Pricing Champion* *(https://amphoraconsulting.com/2023/08/28/five-requirements-to-being-a-value-pricing-champion/)* and *The Important Distinctions Between Value Pricing and Value Selling* (https://www.roi-selling.com/blog/the-important-distinctions-between-value-pricing-and-value-selling?hs_preview=vlnnNfKe-102762568632), I discuss how to incorporate value pricing and value selling into your processes. However, if your offering doesn't create customer value, neither approach will work.

Even market leaders must invest some product development time in "keeping up" with the new features their competitors are offering. If that's all you do, though, over time your product will become a "me too" at best, and maybe worse. You need to do more.

Among all of the improvements you could make, which are the best strategic choices? The key is to focus on those customers in your **target segments** *(https://www.roi-selling.com/blog/three-things-to-do-when-you-target-a-new-market-segment)* are most likely to pay for. In many cases, what your competitors are working on may not be what your target customers will care about or pay for. Likewise, some customer enhancement requests may not create value either.

The best way to determine how much a customer is willing to pay is to estimate, in dollars and cents, how much value the enhancements will create for their business.

How to Use Value to Prioritize Your Roadmap

Use these steps in your evaluation process for both brand new and competitive response feature sets.

- **Step 1** | Determine if the feature is something that your target customers even care about. We have a customer whose offering is intended for B2B companies. There are offerings similar to theirs that are designed for B2C companies. Their first challenge is to not respond to features designed for B2C companies that may not be relevant or important to B2B companies.

- **Step 2** | Estimate, in currency, the size of the problem that the feature set will address. Will it reduce costs, improve labor efficiency, or increase sales revenue? If so, by how much? Where will it impact financial statements? If you don't know, your customer probably doesn't know either.

- **Step 3** | Determine the number of customers in your target segments that actually have the **problem you're solving** *(https://www.roi-selling.com/blog/sell-the-problem-you-solve-not-the-product-you-have)*. Even if it's a problem for one customer, are there enough other customers to make it worth developing the feature set? This will help you evaluate the total market potential for the new capability.

- **Step 4** | Estimate your cost to develop and maintain the feature set. Even if the market potential is five million dollars, it isn't worth doing if it will cost more than a million dollars to deliver it.

- **Step 5** | Prioritize all possible feature sets based on the investment pool available and the potential return on investment that your company could achieve for each initiative.

Tools to Help with Your Analysis

We recommend using these tools to improve the business impact of your product development pipeline. They are listed in order of effectiveness, from least to optimal.

1. **Spreadsheet Analysis of Each New Feature Set**
   Although you can, and many do use spreadsheets to analyze more significant feature sets, it is a lot of work, and it is likely that the analyses are not complete.

2. **Value Calculator for External Use**
   If you have a **value calculator** *(https://www.roi-selling.com/value-calculator)* that your customers use to estimate the business value of your offering, you can also use it to estimate the value of new ideas. Before you do, carefully evaluate whether each value dimension in the existing calculator is applicable to the new feature set. Conversely, estimate the magnitude of impact the new feature set will have on each value dimension.

3. **Value Calculator for Internal Use**
   You can use an existing value calculator that was developed for external use or create a purpose-built calculator to estimate the value of new ideas. With this type of tool, you can explicitly

choose which value dimensions will apply and to what magnitude.

4. **Internal Product Enhancement ROI Tool**

   An excellent approach is to take the value calculator framework described in option 3 and turn it into an **ROI tool** *(https://www.roi-selling.com/roi-tool)* to evaluate new product ideas. In addition to providing the insights obtained in Step 4, you will better understand market potential in terms of the number of customers with the problem. You can also evaluate potential pricing and estimate potential sales. This would then be evaluated against the investment required to develop and maintain the feature set. This approach evaluates the entire business case for the feature set.

5. **Roadmap Portfolio Prioritization Tool**

   The optimal approach is to evaluate each of the business cases developed in the Internal Product Enhancement ROI Tool against each other as a portfolio view. You can then do "what if" scenario planning on different feature sets within the budget available to determine the optimal roadmap.

Conclusion

Prioritizing your product development roadmap using customer value is the best way to optimize your business performance. Leveraging tools to estimate and prioritize product development initiatives is a great way to enable your team to achieve that.

Section 3: Customer Value

Introduction

If there is one concept that distinguishes our approach from the thousands of other pages written on strategy and marketing, it is our insistence on quantifying customer value. The reason lies in our perspective on B2B customers. While consumer markets are heavily influenced by emotion, often even irrational emotion ("drink this beer and you'll be more popular"), B2B buying decisions tend to be based on economics. Said differently, in the long run B2B customers gravitate towards the solutions that are best for their businesses.

As you will read in the following, companies too often assume that their offerings are best for every customer and those who don't buy them are irrational (or 'stupid'). While this may occasionally be true of individual customers (or people at your customers), it cannot possibly be true for a large group of customers – irrational or stupid companies get competed out of business. If a customer appears to be buying something that we don't think is their best option, more often than not, it is because WE do not understand what value really means to them.

Getting value right is complex and nuanced. Too many companies settle for a laundry list of benefits, but value means understanding trade-offs. That is why we insist on quantifying value in currency units. Of course everyone wants durability and energy efficiency, but how much less durable could your offering be if it was 50 percent more energy efficient? Or how much would a customer pay if we could offer improvements in both?

As we say in our workshops, customer value is always customer specific, measured in currency and relative to the next best alternative; but not always easy to understand. Hopefully, the stories in the following help reinforce this key message and help you realize the impact of understanding customer value for your business.

What you need to know about the
value of customer relationships

November 26, 2019

During our grassroots strategy workshops, one of the exercises is to brainstorm a list of things that create (or could create) customer value. Frequently, one of our participants mentions 'relationships.' You probably hear this in other contexts as well: "our value is our customer relationship." In our line of work, certain phrases trigger responses that are instinctive, almost Pavlovian – and for me, this has become one of them. We have heard this so many times and it is almost always incomplete or inaccurate. And worse, it can become something your organization hides behind rather than searching more broadly for customer value.

Let's be clear – we are not anti-relationship. Having strong relationships with your customers is a good thing and is a primary objective of a good sales force – it will help you get repeat business, help you learn about new opportunities ahead of competitors and in many businesses, it may get you 'last look,' that chance to match a competitor's price and steal the business at the last minute. All of these can contribute to a healthier and more profitable business, but while they produce value for you, they are not (directly) valuable to the customer.

When we talk about customer value in Business to Business (B2B) marketing, it must be something that you do uniquely well, that contributes to the customer's bottom line. Value means that you can translate a benefit, for example, 'durability,' into currency: "yes, ours is priced higher up front, but it lasts twice as long so in the long run it is worth it." Customer relationships, as usually defined, fail both parts of this test. Customer relationships are usually defined around individuals, so that your 'relationship' with a customer lasts only as long as the individuals stay in their roles at both your company and theirs. Secondly, it is extremely difficult to translate customer relationships into quantifiable value for the customer.

In our experience, the most notable exception is when the customer is buying something that is hard to define or complicated – at the extreme, the customer may not even understand what they are actually getting – an example might be a large-scale IT project. Here, relationships can be critical because it dramatically limits the risk to the customer if they are dealing with a known provider with a track record for fixing problems and making things work even when the original scope or terms were unclear. Contrast this with a fully specified purchase – if the customer is buying a known service through an RFP process, or ordering standard parts that they buy frequently, the value of a relationship to them is probably close to zero.

One of our clients sold aerospace components and was convinced that their engineer-to-engineer relationships, fostered by their proximity to their largest customer, were a real differentiator. No doubt they had some good relationships, and maybe even some genuine friendships between their salespeople and the customer's engineers. But when the customer changed their buying philosophy to a more purchasing-led approach, the engineers no longer had a voice in the final buying decision and the 'value' of our client's relationships evaporated overnight as they were forced to compete on a level playing field to be 'global best source' (usually interpreted as lowest price that met the spec.) in each category.

In summary, relationships are great – and if you are in sales, that is your primary job: to develop great relationships with your customers, to make sure we get called early and often on every potential opportunity. But if you are thinking strategically about your market and your offerings, relationships are rarely enough. Relying on 'relationships' alone, without understanding what that really means from the customers' perspective, can cause you to overlook potentially more sustainable sources of differentiation and value.

"You Want Me to Pay for That?" – The Myth of 'Customer Requirements'

November 11, 2020

We heard a familiar lament just a couple weeks ago from a VP of Engineering at one of our clients: "If the Sales team would just tell us the customer requirements, we could get on with designing the product." We've heard something similar hundreds of times, and it sounds innocuous at first – what could be wrong with better understanding customer requirements? But we have come to believe that the organizational constructs, processes and frameworks built around 'customer requirements' don't work very well because the very idea is a myth – thinking that there is a precise list of exactly what the customer wants to buy is a dangerous over- simplification of how the world actually works.

A story might help illustrate our point. Several years ago, we were working with a company that makes turbochargers. One critical feature of a turbocharger is 'actuation,' essentially the opening of the valve that allows the turbocharger to function, compressing the incoming air to enable more efficient combustion in the engine.

There are three ways to control actuation: pneumatic, electronic, or pneumatic with electronic position-sensing. The company needed to know which to build into their development plans, as creating a world-class offering in all three types would be prohibitively expensive.

At the time, they were working with one of their largest customers, a major German Auto OEM, on redesigning their 1.6-liter diesel engine design that would utilize a turbocharger. The team contacted their account manager who worked with this customer and had spent hundreds of hours with their engine designers. He was confident that this customer *needed* pneumatic actuation. But when someone on the team asked him 'why?,' the response was a blank stare. Clearly their customer's engineers must be aware of the competing technologies, and they chose pneumatic – what was their thinking?

Somewhat reluctantly, the account manager set up a meeting with the engine designers at the OEM. When it got to the critical question of actuation, the customer engineers began talking about the benefits of a fully electronic system in terms of durability and reliability. The account manager jumped in, "but wait a minute, you told me clearly that for this engine you need a pneumatic actuator. What's going on?" They replied that the immediate need was for pneumatic because their engine control module (the brain that runs the engine) had no available input/output ports. Since anything electronic would require additional i/o ports, those solutions were verboten until the company had spent the tens of millions of Euros to redesign the engine control module. Pneumatic wasn't really their preference – it was a compromise necessitated by something that had nothing to do with turbocharger performance! If our client had bet the future on this 'customer requirement' it would have led them to create an inferior product.

In general, several things are wrong with the concept that the job of the commercial team is simply to tease out customer requirements and document them for the rest of the organization:

- First, customers often don't know what they want. This is not an indictment, rather it reflects the truth that customers are experts in their business not yours – they don't know what they don't know. And lots of research suggests that people are really bad at predicting how they will react to something they have not seen before.

- Customers don't have absolute needs, rather they make trade-offs. We had a client that asked their largest and most important customer what they needed in their next generation product. They replied, "we need it to be 20% lighter, 20% smaller footprint, and 20% cheaper." It wasn't until after our client had built a prototype that they learned that the most important thing was the footprint. In fact, the customer would have accepted a heavier product that cost more for an even smaller footprint –

111

the 20 percent targets were arbitrary design goals.

- Not everyone inside the customer wants the same thing. This may sound obvious, but it can be critical if overlooked. Just ask the suppliers to the automotive industry who spent millions of dollars designing things that the engineering groups at their customers 'needed' only to find that when they talked to purchasing, the required price was last year minus three percent.

- Somewhat related to the previous point, customers will often ask for things that they aren't actually willing to pay for. So, a customer might say that they need an orange-colored display, but how much do they need it? Will they pay $5 for it, or $50 or nothing? Without this more nuanced understanding, how can we know how much to spend on developing that feature? As one of our clients says: almost every problem has a solution, but not every solution has a customer willing to pay for it.

- Not every customer wants the same thing. We have written at length about segmentation, and it is critical here as well. Even if you have perfectly identified the requirements for a given customer, you need to know how many other customers need the same thing before deciding whether it is worth investing in.

- Lastly, even in the rare case where you can document a customer's complete 'spec' for what they will buy, you have probably already lost. If you weren't the one who helped the customer write that spec, it is a safe bet that one of your competitors did. Investing to match what your competitor already offers is just earning you the right to compete on price; and even then, the incumbent probably gets a chance to match.

If the goal is not to document 'customer requirements,' what is it? Our view is that the only way out is to become a student of your customer and their business. This typically requires engaging them outside of the sales process (where they know that everything they say is an input to a negotiation) and really understanding the business trade-offs they face. It is critical to set aside your biases and objectively understand the customer's perspective and the context in which they make decisions and then understand how far we can generalize that perspective.

You will know this is working when everyone across the organization is instinctively asking 'why' questions whenever the idea of customer requirements surfaces and not just jumping immediately to the 'how' do we meet that requirement. Another story highlights how this *should* work:

A company we know makes portable gas detectors. These are small battery-operated devices, typically clipped on the collar of a worker, which detect poisonous gas and emit an audible warning. The device is a regulatory requirement in certain dangerous operating environments, most notably in oil refineries. One of their larger customers has approached our client and asked if they could add a small light indicating a low battery. Thinking that they were being responsive to an important customer, they said 'sure,' and were well on the way to designing in that feature.

While the engineers were busy redrawing the circuitry, a product manager was asked to determine how to price this new feature. Using an approach like we described above, this product manager set out to understand why this customer wanted a low battery indicator and figure out what they might pay for it. Walking the customer through a day in their life (clearly not part of a sales negotiation), they discovered that the value was potentially quite large. Workers are not allowed to work with a non-functioning detector, so when a battery dies, they either ignore it, which is both a safety and compliance issue, or they stop working and walk back to a base station where they can get a new detector. This was a major productivity issue at a refinery with hundreds of workers spread over sometimes dozens of square miles, and almost certainly an issue that would be relevant to lots of customers, not just this one.

Armed with this more nuanced understanding of the customer needs, the product manager designed a complete solution that would provide their customers with spare detectors, battery charging stations and software that ensured that each worker left their base with a working detector that would last through their shift. In addition, the system would automatically document compliance if their customer was ever audited. The result was that our client was able to capture an additional $30 per detector – far more than the $2-3 per detector that engineering was originally thinking based on the relatively small cost of adding the indicator light.

Thinking beyond 'customer requirements' is not easy. It may require new skills to generate the required market insight, and it typically means an ongoing and robust two-way dialogue between commercial and technical teams, not a one-time hand-off of a requirements spec, as it is often conceptualized. But as these stories indicate, getting it wrong can be disastrous and getting right can lead to exciting new opportunities to create value in ways you or your customers have not even imagined!

Why Won't Those Stupid Customers Buy My Valuable Solution?

May 24, 2022

"We could grow faster if those stupid customers just understood the real value of our solution." If we had a dollar for every time we have heard a client say some version of that, we would be rich. The problem with that line of thinking is that it is a dead end. If customers are stupid, and knowingly buying something other than their best option, then what hope do we have of changing that?

We have come to believe that the 'stupid customers' line of thinking is a convenient, but at best superficial, explanation for not making a sale. The truth is that individual customers may seem stupid – they certainly make decisions that we don't understand. But whole segments of customers are not systematically stupid, or they wouldn't still be in business. Nearly always, a better explanation is that we have failed to fully understand value from the customer's perspective. Too often we see companies who:

- Focus on value to themselves, not value to the customer ("we want to sell more high-end product")

- Assume that their offering is the best alternative for every customer, without applying thoughtful segmentation.

- Are good at talking to customers but may not be good at listening to them.

- Frame the customer problem from their perspective without thinking through the trade-offs the customer faces as a business (best technical solution versus best way to solve the business problem)

Example Situation

As always, an example helps to illustrate this point. We recently worked with a client that produces an additive that reduces the processing cost for certain types of polymer-based products. They had a profitable business and had been quite successful when they were involved early in the product design and qualification process. They had demonstrated that they could help their direct customers meet their end-customers' product specifications while reducing the cost of producing the product.

Their frustration came when trying to convert customers with existing products to their additive. They knew that substituting their additive would lower a customer's production cost, yet they could not get them to switch. What was wrong with these 'stupid' customers?

Failed Attempts

Their sales force treated this as an objection to overcome and they rolled out different messaging and various commercial programs designed to get customers to switch. Thinking that it was a cash or capital problem, they had tried various financing programs. This still didn't move the needle in terms of more customers adopting.

They tried to fund pilot trials. They offered to support the engineering effort to reformulate and provide free samples for evaluation testing. Still very few takers. So, what was wrong? What were they missing?

Understanding their customers economics

We forced them to step back and dig into their customers' economics, not just the economics of producing the material, but the full end-to-end cost implications of designing, producing, qualifying, and delivering the material to their customers – the one-time expenses that economists would call "switching costs." It turned out that in most cases the qualification process that end-customers required started all the way back at the design stage. They were involved in every step, from approving the formulation, approving the processing method, and then qualifying that the material actually met their specification.

In order to even initiate the change, they had to engage their customer (or more often than not, multiple customers) to even start the process. They would then have to disrupt their production to produce samples and support the end-customers through a lengthy qualification process. The cost of going through this process was in the hundreds of thousands of dollars, often approaching a million. So, while the eventual savings to the customer were real, when they ran the numbers the way a customer would, the payback on the switching costs was typically five years or more. These customers weren't stupid – they were making exactly the right decision for them, given their limited resources.

Results

After investing to understand their customers' economics, our client dramatically changed their approach to the market. They found that not all applications had this stringent and costly material qualification process. Some end-customers (typically outside of automotive and aerospace) did not even require notification for a change in formulation, as long as the product still worked. Our client developed a focused Go-To-Market plan around these applications (aka segments) where the processing cost reduction far outweighed the switching cost (aka customer value), and not only increased their success, but reduced their selling cost, because they were no longer wasting time trying to persuade customers where they were not their best option.

Summary

If you are struggling to get customers to change what they are already doing, don't assume they are making a bad decision. It is crucial in those cases to understand their underlying economic incentives in order to determine if your offering really creates value. By honestly evaluating the entire economic picture you can better understand both the value your offering can create and identify the areas where your offering could be destroying value (like switching costs). Then, armed with that knowledge, you may be able to find segments of customers where those negatives are not as significant.

Failing to step back and think about the market systematically and objectively is an example of what we have called the strategy 'short-circuit.': assuming that your challenge is to educate customers on why they should buy your offering without thinking through the basics of segmentation, value and differentiation. Effective market strategy starts with listening, not talking, to develop an informed view of customer needs.

Remember, it is highly likely that your customers are acting in their own best interest. So, if they don't do what you would expect, you probably need to dig deeper to understand and frame the decision from their perspective.

"Anyone, Anyone?" Who's Thinking about Economics?

July 11, 2023

If you follow pop culture even a little bit, you recognize the reference in our title to Ben Stein's portrayal of the boring economics teacher in **_Ferris Bueller's Day Off_** _(https://www.youtube.com/watch?v=uhiCFdWeQfA)._

Like the high school class staring vacantly as Stein's character explains the Smoot-Hawley Tariff and the Laffer Curve*, many of our clients fail to thoroughly consider economics, assuming that it is just financial calculations that should be left to the accounting department.

The scene works because economics is generally considered to be boring. Maybe this is because it is taught poorly, or maybe it has something to do with the terrible track record of macro-economic predictions. In any case, while most businesspeople have taken at least some economics, they tend to leave it behind at university like those nearly forgotten courses in psychology and sociology. Worse yet, many senior managers adopt the language of accountants when describing their businesses, sidestepping a real economic understanding of how their market and their business actually work.

Before we back up this assertion, let's start with a definition. Microeconomics is the science dedicated to understanding how individuals and companies make trade-offs among scarce resources. Since nearly all- important decisions involve trade-offs and every important resource eventually becomes scarce, microeconomics is in essence a way of understanding how people and companies make decisions.

When it comes to the subset of people and companies that you want to be your customers, building this understanding is key. It is microeconomics that gives us the tools to unlock the code, building an informed and

objective view of how customers make trade-offs. While there are other ways to *describe* how your customers make decisions, we would argue strongly that economic thinking is by far the best way to *predict* what they will buy when faced with a hypothetical set of options (e.g., how much business will we lose if we raise prices ten percent? How much more can we charge if we add this new feature? Accounting is silent on these topics).

To be clear, good accounting is important. We need an accurate record of how much we sold and how much profit we made, and certainly we need to accurately calculate our taxes. But accounting is historical, not forward looking. When we use accounting terms and assumptions to make projections, it can lead us to bad business decisions.

One example that comes to mind is the phrase 'margin dilution.' Managers trained in accountant-speak throw this term about as if it is always a bad thing. It is true that if your business model is not changing declining margins on steady sales are almost always bad; it is typically a symptom of either a loss of pricing power (commoditization) or increases in costs. But when it comes to forward-looking business decisions, 'dilution' is not the right way to think about it.

For example, if your base business delivers 12 percent operating income (OI), should you turn down a $1 billion order at ten percent OI because it will dilute earnings? With accountant thinking, the answer would be to avoid this order, but is that always the right decision?

A business leader grounded in economics might start by making sure that the cost was calculated correctly to estimate the profitability of this new order. Accountants love to allocate overheads and use average costs. But if this order is incremental, the right cost to consider is the 'marginal cost,' probably much closer to the true variable cost. Depending on the nature of your business, this may be very different than what is shown on the COGS (Cost of Goods Sold) line of your income statement, as this contains allocated fixed costs.

The next step is to frame the relevant options – the choice this hypothetical business faces is not 'do I want this.

$1 billion order at 10 percent or another $1billion of base business at 12 percent?' That answer is as obvious as that question is wrong. And certainly, if we can win the new business at a higher price and get the margin up to 12 percent that is good. But assuming that we have negotiated well, and the 10 percent reflects a 'take it or leave it' price, then the relevant question is "should I take this business that is available or not, and what will happen if I decline to bid and the business goes to my competitor?" This answer does not pop out of a spreadsheet, rather it requires an in-depth understanding of how customers and competitors think – in our words, what are their economics? How do they make trade-offs? What is their cost structure? Etc.

Some of the key differences in thinking like an accountant vs. an economist are summarized in the table below:

Accounting	Economics
• Historical	• Forward looking
• Account for what happened	• Compare opportunities
• Numbers depend on the purpose of the accounting (tax, regulation, debt, SEC, control, decision-making, etc.)	• Numbers depend on the quality of sources…and their purpose is to support decision-making
	• Fixed and variable costs
• Direct and indirect costs	
	• Marginal costs
• Total and average costs	• Opportunity costs
• Allocation	• Capital costs
• Absorption	

Economic thinking is the foundation of our approach to customer value and market segmentation. It is critical to understanding your markets and finding and prioritizing opportunities. If you are not thinking like an economist, don't assume that anyone else is – said differently, economics is too important to be left to the accountants. The business stakes are high – if you fail to understand economics, you may find yourself asleep and drooling on your desk, while your competitors find new ways to add value for customers and gradually eat away at your market share.

*The back story is that the economics teacher character had very few scripted
121

lines, but Mr. Stein, who is an economist (and a lawyer) in addition to being an actor, ad-libbed most of the lecture that made the final cut of the movie, and for many movie geeks, created one of the more memorable scenes is this iconic film.

Section 4: Segmentation and Value Proposition

Introduction

One of our customers explained segmentation in a powerful way. She said "what we are looking for with segmentation is groups of customers that really need what we do well and their next best alternative is ugly and expensive." What a powerful strategy if you can find those customers!

The key to finding segments of customers that fit that definition is to start with customer needs, and more specifically customer needs that map to your unique differentiators – you cannot do this if your segmentation efforts stop at buying a report based on how everyone else segments the market. The best segmentations find groups of customers that have a similar set of needs that can be solved by your offering. It also should identify groups of customers where you may not be their best option, or at least segments where you don't want to spend too much time trying to serve.

Once you have identified those groups of customers, it should be quite straightforward to develop segment specific value propositions for each group you plan to target. A good value proposition shouldn't be a superficial list of features or attributes, but a quantified statement of how you will solve problems and deliver value to your customers. It also should serve as the guidebook for the entire organization to stay focused on what is important to deliver on that value proposition.

Segmentation is a messy process and there are more ways to get it wrong than there are effective segmentations. The following articles highlight some of our tips and tricks to effective segmentation as well as some cautionary tales on things to avoid.

Market Segmentation – Why is it so Difficult?

July 9, 2020

In our Grassroots Strategy workshops with clients, the highlight of the week is often market segmentation. Done well, it is one of the most important changes in the way you think about your business and customers – the customers you choose to serve and how you serve them impacts both the revenue and the expense sides of your income statement. But too often, teams struggle to do it well.

Like 'strategy,' 'segmentation' is one of those words that almost every company uses but can mean very different things to different companies. Some companies refer to business segments, others may mean product lines, still others label customer end-use industry or vertical market as a 'segment.' Many companies have an account segmentation of "key" customers and "transactional" customers. We even remember one client who told us sincerely that they had two segments: smart customers who bought from them and stupid customers who didn't!

Some of these classifications may be helpful in tracking your business. But, in our experience, to get the full power from using segmentation– the only thing that works is segmentation grounded in customer needs.

A good needs-based segmentation allows you to tailor your offering to specific segment needs including:

- Development of specific products

- Providing different levels of support

- Allocating different levels of sales resources

- Using different channels and pricing differently based on the specific value created for that segment.

Tailoring your offering to target segments and pricing to value improves the revenue line through both greater volume and higher margin. Focusing resources on segments where you are most advantaged impacts the expense line by reducing unproductive sales activity and by avoiding over-featuring an offering for segments where these features are not valued.

The basic concept is fairly simple, almost obvious: "different customers have different needs, so let's put them into some logical groupings and develop different approaches for each group." And yet, many struggle to make this work in practice. So, what is it about needs-based segmentation that makes it so difficult?

We have identified five things that get in the way of effective B2B market segmentation:

1. **Lack of Strategic Marketing Capability** – Good segmentation requires a strategic marketing capability. Too many B2B companies are sales-centric, with little or no marketing beyond marketing communications. Having a great salesforce is important, but it is not enough. Left to their own, salespeople tend to believe "every customer is a good customer" and "every customer is different." While not completely untrue, this way of thinking can inhibit getting to a workable segmentation. Different customers have different cost of sales, value our offering differently and have differing probability of choosing us over our competition. This results in different customers having differing profitability. While technically, "every customer *is* different", customizing everything for every customer is rarely the right approach. Grouping customers with similar needs is an extremely powerful tool to drive your business and focus your resources.

2. **Desire to Quantify** – Too many companies, especially those that are technologically strong, instinctively believe that you don't know something unless you know it exactly. This causes them to tend to focus on segmenting based on data that are readily available and to reach for statistical techniques that will produce precise answers, but these segmentations are often not helpful.

    a) For example, they may require detailed data that only exists for current customers, meaning that we have no way of putting non-customers into the segmentation and thereby finding new ways to engage them. As if walking you into this trap, several analytics firms are happy to tell their clients that this statistical approach is the only way to do segmentation.

b) A segmentation framework based on strategically actionable needs (even if it resists precise quantification) is much more powerful than a precisely quantified segmentation that does no more than describe the existing market using available data.

3. **Incorrectly Applying Consumer Segmentation Techniques –** Consumer segmentation often uses psychographics to gain insight into how end-customers think about the product or problem and how it fits into their lifestyle. This can be quite important in consumer messaging, for example in being able to separate the hard core DIY'er who enjoys tackling home remodeling projects from their neighbor who might reluctantly undertake an occasional home repair project to save a few dollars. They may buy the same product, but their motivation and response to retail promotions would be very different. This emphasis on 'personas' is easily misapplied in a B2B context. And, if the end-customer being studied is not the primary decision-maker, it may be downright misleading.

a) As an example, one of our clients sold residential entry doors. They did a detailed study of consumer attitudes about their front door and the perceived value it brought to their home. The work was interesting, but extremely difficult to link to the buying process, where the vast majority of doors are purchased as part of a larger project (often a new construction house) and the customer's choice is bounded by what the contractor offers – which in the extreme may be just a choice of paint color.

b) While individual end-consumers do make some buying decisions, the ultimate buyer in the B2B world is the purchasing business entity. Segmentation is generally most productive when based on the functional and economic needs of the business entity, not the emotional/psychographic attitudes of the individual end- consumers. Linking segmentation to the reality of the purchase decision process is essential.

4. **Lack of Deep Customer Insight** – Many B2B companies are short-term oriented and sometimes overly focused on the channel customer (the one who can take an extra truckload to help them make the quarter) rather than customers further down the value chain. Too often, these companies lack the insight required to factor end-customer needs into their segmentation, at the extreme, if they sell through a distributor, formulator or converter, they may not even know who the end-customer is. Building an objective view further into the value chain is almost always worthwhile (who is the end-customer and what are the problems they are trying to solve?). Some combination of systematic observation and targeted VOC can yield a huge payback and is a prerequisite to developing a workable segmentation.

5. **Not willing to Face the Implications** – Some of our clients have a reasonable segmentation, but it exists only as a PowerPoint chart somewhere in the marketing department – there is no process to actually change what they offer or how they price or serve a customer based on the segment into which they fall. Said differently, if the only answer that sales will accept is "every customer gets two sales calls a year and buys from the same price list," then segmentation is a waste of time. Impactful segmentation has to drive organization-wide change in which customers you serve and how you interact with them through sales, distribution, technical support and customer service – it can't just be a marketing exercise.

We have found that segmentation is always iterative and sometimes messy. Segmentation is part art and part science – there is no process diagram that always produces the right answer on a fixed timetable. In fact, it is unlikely that there is one 'right answer' – you can usually tell that one segmentation is more helpful than another, but that doesn't guarantee that there might not be a better one waiting to be discovered. For that reason, we like to leave the working sessions on segmentation open-ended, and on occasion they have gone well into the night.

Segmentation is hard work but extremely rewarding when you get it right. In an upcoming blogpost, "Market Segmentation – How to get it Right?", we will describe some of the principles and techniques we use to avoid the mistakes above and unleash the power of an effective needs-based segmentation.

Market Segmentation – How to Get it Right

August 7, 2020

We continue to believe that done well, market segmentation is not just a critical marketing tool but can be the defining element of your overall strategy. In our previous blog post, we shared the most common difficulties in getting to a workable needs-based segmentation. So, what can you do to avoid those mistakes and unleash the power of an effective segmentation? There is no easy answer, but here a few things to keep in mind as you work as you work through this critical task:

- Segment at the right level – Insightful segmentations are generally at the lowest level of the value chain that you can make actionable. If you are selling automotive parts to car manufacturers, for example, you might get some insight from segmenting car purchasers, but it would be difficult to act on this directly. It is certainly more actionable to segment automotive OEMs, since they are your direct customers; but even that may not be sufficient – BMW likely has different needs for a diesel sedan built in Germany than for an electric vehicle built in the US – so application or platform might be the right way to segment.

- Segment with an eye towards your differentiation – remember, winning strategies are found in your sweet- spots, those intersections of under-met customer needs with things you do uniquely well. So, the right segmentation for you is not the right segmentation for your competitors. Starting with an understanding of your differentiation and then exploring why some customers value it a lot and others very little is a great way to start…

- … Building on that, fewer needs are generally better – segmentation works best when you can zero in on the couple of customer needs that really determine whether or not you can win in that segment. Starting with a long list of universal needs can add unnecessary noise to the process. Worse yet, there is what we've come to call the 2^N problem. Stated

129

simply, if you have N different needs and a given customer can be high or low on that need, then you have 2^N potential segments. No matter how theoretically pure this approach feels, if N is anything greater than three, you almost always end up with an unworkable number of segments. The sooner you can agree on the two to three needs that really matter, the smoother the process will be.

• Use 'why?' questions to match customer characteristics to needs – Don't confuse customer characteristics with needs. Only a distinct set of needs defines a segment. But segmentation works best when we can identify a link between characteristics and needs. The key usually starts with 'why?' questions. For example:

Q: Why do some customers value technical support more than others?

A: Because some customers have experienced internal engineering groups, and some don't (reason behind the need)

Q: Which customers do not have experienced internal engineering?

A: Usually, those are start-ups with fewer than 200 employees (company characteristic)

Q: Why don't start-ups have internal engineering?

A: Usually, they have been focused on driving the revenue side of their business through design and have outsourced value engineering (the logic that links the need to the characteristic)

• Accept the imperfect – good segmentations do not need to be exact. In fact, it is okay to have an 'all other' segment for that last 10 or 15 percent of the market that doesn't fall neatly into a category. The key to making segmentation actionable is basing it on information that you can know before you go on a sales call. That is the only way to proactively tailor your communications, your offering and potentially your price. You may guess wrong sometimes as to which segment a specific customer falls into, but as long as you collect the feedback you can adjust as you go. A segmentation need not be perfect to be useful, as long as you recognize that segmentation is iterative, and building the feedback mechanisms to adapt over time.

- Focus on the implications – Sometimes when teams really struggle with how to segment, we flip the problem on its head and start with implications – what are you willing to do differently across segments? Change service levels, develop custom products, charge different prices? If you can answer this question clearly, sometimes you can get to a segmentation indirectly. For example, by asking why you would be willing to provide a higher service level for some customers than others. This type of 'reverse engineering' can often shed light on the customer characteristics and needs that should be defining our segmentation approach. If nothing else, it forces your team to realize that segmentation is not just a mental exercise for internal reporting.

All of these recommendations also highlight the importance of involving a cross-functional team – consistent with how we think about strategy, there is no monopoly on good ideas. So, involving more functions and perspectives in the segmentation process is almost always a good idea. At a minimum, it will prevent groupthink and help avoid creating a segmentation that looks good on paper but cannot be implemented. This tends to be true because involving people outside the marketing department will force the, sometimes awkward, discussion on implications – what will actually be different if we implement this segmentation and are we comfortable doing that?

As a last piece of advice, and perhaps the most important of all, don't give up. Segmentation is hard and takes concerted, cross-functional effort that does not come natural to many companies, especially those who have historically been driven by sales and/or technical excellence and may not understand or value strategic marketing. But taking the time to do segmentation properly is almost always worth it. For those who get it right it can be the centerpiece of their strategy and position them for ongoing success.

Good Segmentation Schemes Often
Start Out Sounding 'Just Crazy Enough'

September 29, 2021

Making Sense of the Messy Middle

"It just takes some time Little girl, you're in the middle of the ride Everything, everything will be just fine Everything, everything will be all right, all right."

~The Middle by Jimmy Eat World

One of the benefits of having coached project teams through our needs-based segmentation process hundreds of times across dozens of industries is that we can spot patterns that are difficult to identify for even the seasoned industry practitioner who has typically developed a limited number of segmentation schemes, probably in just one or two industries. One pattern that we often see is a natural clustering of customers based on size and complexity – with large customers demanding a high degree of customization for their unique requirements and small customers buying just one or two standard products serving their far simpler needs (or if they do have greater needs, we cannot afford to serve them because of their purchase volume).

While this type of segmentation works in addressing those two extremes, the problem is 'the middle' – the medium-size, medium complexity customers. Leaving them all in one segment is often not a good option, as they can comprise 60 – 70 percent of your revenue. Trying to further refine them along these two dimensions, by creating 'small-mediums' and 'medium-larges' for example, might be initially satisfying, but it is usually not informative in terms of changing segment strategies, and it can be misleading.

We have always said that segmentation is messy and iterative. So, if you run into this type of situation, don't give up. Or as the song says, "don't write yourself off yet." Remember that in segmentation, we are looking to exploit asymmetries – the underlying factors that drive different needs among otherwise similar customers. Here are some things to consider when trying to tease out important differences in these medium customers:

- First, ask yourself if you have the right segmentation variables. While size and complexity may seem initially appealing, do they really explain customer purchasing behavior and underlying needs? Step back and ask yourself what are the key differences in needs relative to your offering that we might exploit in a segment- based strategy. Explore other possible segmentation variables that might better explain differences in needs, such as: business model (i.e., innovator vs. follower) or step in value chain (i.e., Tier 1 or Integrated OEM). While you may have already invested in developing size and complexity as a way to segment your markets, don't settle on a segmentation framework unless it clearly ties to underlying needs.

- Second, make sure you are thinking about all potential customers and the whole customer, not just taking an internal view of what we sell today. Too often, segmentation starts with internal sales data. Obviously, this gives you no visibility to customers who don't buy from us. But more importantly, for this topic, you may define a customer as medium when in fact we represent only 20 percent of their purchases. They may actually be a large customer who only values us as a secondary supplier. Their needs and the implications for how we serve them might be very different than those of a truly medium-sized customer where we have 100 percent of their business.

- Third, if you keep coming back to size and complexity, see if you can further define these segmentation variables. Size and complexity can be interpreted fairly broadly. You get a deeper insight if you add some granularity to these definitions. For example, is size based on number of people, square footage of facility or number of locations rather than just annual purchase volume? This can be important, as purchases are an outcome while these other characteristics are often one step closer to the underlying need. The same is true on the complexity dimension, is it number of product lines purchased, number and variety of sensor inputs or frequency of changes to the system? All of these can contribute to complexity, but the implications may be very different.

- Fourth, see if there is some other structural dimension that you can add to the segmentation framework that might tease out differences within the "messy middle". Is there another dimension along which customers vary that could be driving differences in needs and therefore buying behavior? For example, two customers may be similar in their technical product requirements, but one is a mature company with an experienced engineering group that does their own integration while the other is a start-up with limited experience who needs to buy a turnkey system and a support contract in order to accomplish the same end. In this case, adding a dimension of technical maturity to your segmentation framework might be powerful and more directly linked to needs.

- Lastly, think beyond the product to see if sub-groups of these middle customers might be served by a different business model. For example, if you could make your product easier to self-configure or re-package your offering 'as a service' which customers would be most interested in it and why? This thought exercise may help better identify and define differences of underlying needs within the messy middle. Are there additional services that some customers might be willing to pay for but that others would not? This is always a good sign that you are getting closer to an actionable segmentation.

To see how these can all come together to create a real insight, we recall a client of ours who sold Personal Protective Equipment (PPE) to industrial facilities around the world. They quickly saw that their customers followed the size/complexity pattern we have described here. They had very large, demanding customers who wanted custom programs and products and shopped their PPE spend in large and very detailed multi-year tenders that required aggressive pricing to win. At the other extreme were small customers who bought only one or two categories of PPE at volumes that were most economically served on-line – no personally selling, customization or discounting made sense for this segment.

The problem was that these two extremes combined described just over 30 percent of their potential business – the vast majority of their sales (and even more of their profit margin) came from the medium-size/medium- complexity 'middle.' As they dug deeper, they realized that they had lumped into this medium bucket some customers with a single relatively large location and other customers, with a similar annual purchase volume, but spread across many individually small facilities.

This turned out to be a critical distinction because large single sites usually have a dedicated Environmental Health and Safety (EHS) Manager. These managers generally viewed themselves as the PPE expert – they knew their facility, did their research, defined exactly what they wanted and how much they would buy. They typically tried to play vendors off against one another in a process that was fairly similar to what we described for 'large' customers.

On the other hand, the medium customer with multiple small sites likely had just one EHS manager serving all of them. Many of these customers would value a supplier who could help them track the different regulatory requirements across facilities, set up inventory management programs to make sure key items never go out of stock, and provide summarized usage and compliance reports. All of these are additional services that represented incremental revenue opportunities for our client and would also help make them 'stickier' as a supplier with this newly identified segment. So, if you find yourself stuck in the middle, you could do a lot worse than to take the advice of Jimmy Eat World: "Just do your best. Do everything you can. And don't you worry what their bitter hearts are gonna say." Go back and try the suggested paths above: maybe you are too internally focused, maybe your segmentation variables are wrong, maybe you need to further define your segmentation variables, maybe you need to add a dimension. In our experience, there is almost always a way to subsegment this messy middle, if you are willing to step out of comfort zone and try something different. Remember, segmentation is an iterative process and good segmentation schemes, like good strategies, often start out sounding 'just crazy enough.'

Five Pointers to Avoid Being Stuck in a Segment

November 4, 2021

Applying Grassroots Strategy and pursuing properly structured Voice of the Customer is a great way to grow your business and avoid being stuck in a single segment or worse yet stuck in the wrong segment.

Grassroots Strategy is a powerful conceptual framework, it changes how many of our clients think and leads to exciting new ways for them to conceptualize their businesses. After having worked with our client teams to crack the code in applying key concepts like differentiation, customer value and market segmentation, it often strikes us that the module on Voice of the Customer (VOC) taught towards the end of the workshop could seem a bit mundane.

In truth, the name VOC is a bit of a misnomer. In the past, we have attempted to change the name of this module to "Voice of the Market" or "Market Insight" but for whatever reason "Voice of The Customer "always seems to come back, despite the fact that we are describing something far larger and more important than an annual survey of existing customers that is sometimes also labelled "VOC."

Whatever the name, we include VOC in our training because in our experience, one of the major failure modes in applying strategic marketing is lack of market insight. However smart you might be in applying strategic marketing frameworks and developing hypotheses based on past experience, you will likely fail if you do not have the requisite understanding of the market.

Too many clients stop short of doing the sometimes-challenging work to develop an independent and objective view of how customers actually think and why. This would be like a scientist developing a theory, but never bothering to develop a test to confirm it – no self-respecting journal would publish such shoddy work. But this shortcut is tragically commonplace in the corporate world where there is always something perceived as more urgent than better market insight.

For that reason, in our workshops, after we have worked with our teams to apply the key concepts of market definition, differentiation, customer value and segmentation to their projects, we typically work with them to develop a detailed VOC plan. Good plans include who to talk to, how to approach them (the 'cover story'), how to structure the actual VOC discussion and how to document and share the results of these discussions.

Often when planning whom to speak with we are asked, "Should we only speak with current customers, or do we need to speak with non-customers too?" Early on we were surprised by this question, but unfortunately, we hear it far too often. For the record, the answer to this question is an emphatic "Yes!" Talking only to existing customers is certainly easier to arrange. Talking to non-customers, on the other hand, can be a bit scary. We may not know the person or people in the right roles and when we do find them, we may not like what we hear. But including non-customers in your VOC plans is absolutely essential because:

- When selling to businesses the critical decision maker is often not your direct customer but your customer's customer. For example, for a Tier 2 automotive supplier the key direct customers are the tier one suppliers they serve. But, in order to think through a product road map and value proposition they will need to understand customer value where it is generated and this may be several steps down the value chain, in this example at the OEM or even End User. It is essential to incorporate the perspective of these 'customers' even if you may never sell to them directly.

- Growing with existing customers is great, but step-change growth in your business is likely to come from the parts of the market that you don't currently serve. How can we expect to grow the business if we don't understand the parts of the market where much of the growth could emerge?

- Finally, even if it wasn't intentional, it is likely that your current customers

137

are all in a specific segment or two. Even if you have not done the hard work of segmentation, your customers have likely self-selected such that your current customers are in the segments that need your current value proposition(s). If you do not reach out to understand non-customers, you will continue to only understand one or two segments of the market. The segments you currently serve by default may not be the right segments for you or at least may not be the segments with the most growth opportunity.

Speaking only with your current customers and not your non-customers may be symptomatic of a bigger issue of being stuck in a segment and possibly stuck in the wrong segment. One of our major clients was a Global Telecom Technology Business. In the early stages of mobile telephony, they flourished by helping develop and scale some of the major mobile networks in Europe and the US. When we first came across them, they had offices in two Western European Capitals and maintained relationships with many of the major Western European Telecom companies. Unfortunately, they had very little business in Europe and their gross profit did not even cover their cost of sales. While they had strong businesses in Asia, Africa and South America they were losing money in Europe.

Their European sales activity consisted of an endless cycle of chasing and losing large bids to major Telecom companies who were no longer interested in the company's superior technology, willingness to solve complex customer problems and willingness to customize. Instead, the major Telecom networks wanted high volumes of standard products and low prices. The sales force blamed their lack of success on the company's cost structure, which did not allow them to compete at the price levels required by this customer set.

When a new management team came in, they insisted on a VOC effort to sort out the European business. The sales force reached out to their current customers and the results of this first pass of VOC confirmed what they had been telling management, their prices were too high and customers were not willing to pay for the company's superior offerings.

Some in the management team suspected that the problem was that they were talking to the wrong segment and suggested that the regional organization broaden its VOC to include non-customers. After much kicking and screaming, the European team conducted a broader VOC effort and discovered that while the major players had driven commoditization with their competitive bidding approach, there were several smaller but growing.

 segments that would pay a premium for the company's superior technology and support services. As a result, the company began shifting its commercial resources to these growing segments. It seems obvious after the fact that the company had been stuck in the wrong segment – admiring the problem rather than redefining the boundaries to find a different customer segment.

This recalls the old joke that we re-tell in Grassroots Strategy: "about a police officer slowly making his rounds in the wee hours of the morning. He comes upon a disheveled man in a deserted parking lot, crawling around on his hands and knees in the circle of light created by a lone streetlamp. The police officer gets out of his squad car, approaches the man, and asks him what he is doing. The man, who has obviously been drinking, responds that he is looking for his car keys. When the officer asks if he lost them near this location, the drunk replies, "No, I dropped them back there near the bar, but the light is better here.""

The point is that this company, and many others we have seen, was only looking where it was easiest and most comfortable, not looking where they are most likely to find their target. We have the following five pointers for how to avoid being stuck in a customer segment or stuck in the wrong customer segment:

- Periodically step out of your current business to rethink your segmentation and your value proposition, purposefully thinking from the customer's perspective.

- Keep a broad market view beyond only your current customer set. Specifically get into the habit of consistently monitoring an expanded market definition including VOC with non-customers.

- Do objective 'post-mortem' analysis on lost customers and deals, as a forcing function to see how current offerings might need to be adjusted (dismissing these as stupid customers who made the wrong decision is a symptom of continuing to look only under the streetlamp).

- Make sure your sales incentives encourage your sales force to develop and penetrate new customers in target segments and not just continue to collect orders from your existing relationships.

- Consider creating a 'red team' or some other form of war gaming to better understand why competitors might view the market or segments differently than you do.

Of course a great way to refresh and broaden your understanding of the market is through one of Amphora's Grassroots Strategy Workshops but our main message here is to make sure not to get stuck in the wrong segment and, when doing VOC to broaden your understanding of the market, make sure to reach beyond your current customer base!

Segmentation Is Never Easy, It's Iterative

October 30, 2023

When we conduct our Grassroots Strategy workshops, we are sometimes asked why we dive deep into customer value before we do segmentation. Isn't value segment specific? Shouldn't we define segments independent of what we offer today? We have come to believe that these questions reflect a common misunderstanding that segmentation should be exclusively market back. In other words, we should throw away any references to our existing business or preconceived notions about the how the market works and seek to identify "pure" segments unencumbered by biases associated with our previous participation in the market. But this argument is wrong on several levels:

- It assumes that segments "exist" before we identify them.

- It ignores one of the key objectives of segmentation which is actionability.

- It overlooks the potential to drive a game–changing strategy – by segmenting based on our differentiation rather than looking outside-in at the market.

So, what is a segment anyway? Everyone generally agrees that segments are groups of customers with common needs. But customers have a multitude of needs which means we can segment the market in an infinite number of ways depending on which needs we choose to group customers around. Because there are so many different ways to segment customers (so many different needs we might segment on), there is no way to define the "right" way to segment the market. That having been said, the point of segmenting the market is to determine a course of action that will allow us to grow in parts of the market attractive to us, focus our resources on the right value propositions for those segments and out position our competition who may be treating the market on average.

While there is no way to determine if a segmentation framework is right, we can say that a segmentation is a "good" segmentation only if it is strategically actionable. Clearly segmentation should be based on the needs of customers and not based on our own products or channels. But segmentation can't be based on just any needs, it has to be based on customer needs relevant to our current or potential offering. We would argue that without an understanding of customer needs relative to our differential value it is almost impossible to get to a segmentation that is strategically actionable. Remember, in B2B markets good segmentations are based on asymmetries in the underlying economics of potential customers – e.g., why would some pay a lot more than others for the same offering/value proposition?

Further, while we encourage teams to begin building a value calculation model early in the strategic marketing process, too often people try to skip this step. Often teams are uncomfortable with the 'funny math' with what can seem like almost made-up numbers. But, understanding the relative magnitude of different value elements early on helps parse through what areas of our offering are most important to the customer. In turn this helps us better understand impactful ways to segment our customers.

On a recent project we were helping a pollution control company think through the opportunity for control of certain pollutant gases in the context increasing regulation. They had a chemical-based system while traditional competitors used relatively standard thermal oxidation. There were several benefits of their chemical-based system:

- Chemical-based systems can be safer because they operate at lower temperatures.

- The chemical-based system cost effectively treats the pollutant gases at lower concentrations.

- The chemical-based system reaches close to 100% pollutant destruction while thermal oxidation often only reached 98%.

- Chemical-based systems typically take up less space.

It turns out that there was a lot of data on the pollutant sources. Based on this data, several segmentation frameworks were proposed:

- Size of the source

- Industrial process at source

- Space available at the source

- Location of the source

- Number of gas streams at the source

- Ownership of the source

The client launched a comprehensive VOC process to better understand the pollutant sources and better understand how to segment the market. They focused mainly on the largest emitters of the pollutant and therefore sources that emitted the highest concentrations of the pollutant in their gas streams. They found out that most industrial sources cared about safety, were worried about evolving legislation and were looking for cost effective ways to control emissions They also found out that the pollutant emissions were, to a certain extent, a function of the specific industrial process and that most industrial sources had a lot of space available. Everyone they spoke with expressed interest in any potential new technology. But there was no apparent impactful way to segment the market.

Midway through the project they finally built a value model of how lifecycle costs of chemical-based technologies compared to thermal oxidation across different parameters. They discovered that the overwhelming driver of the competitiveness of their solution was the concentration of the pollutant in the gas being treated. At very low concentrations no technology is cost effective, at mid-range concentration levels their solution is clearly the best financial option, while at high concentrations thermal oxidation is more cost effective. With this insight it started to become much clearer how to segment the market and where to focus.

Had they had this insight before they started the VOC, they could well have decided to include in their VOC more customers in the middle range of concentration and they may have investigated and probed a different set of issues in these VOC conversations. In fact, mid-way through the process, the company did refocus their VOC efforts around these new insights.

Eventually their final segmentation framework was more nuanced and included, not only the concentration of the gas being treated, but also the regulatory framework based on the source location. This segmentation framework allowed them to focus both their technological development as well as their commercial activities on the middle concentration segment. Their new segmentation was clear and actionable and came from an understanding of the market based on needs relative to their differentiation and where their offering would create the most value. The key insight came from understanding value from the customer perspective and, in particular, actually developing the value equation in parallel to exploring a potential segmentation.

It is for this reason and for others that, in our Grassroots Strategy Framework, we put customer value before segmentation. To avoid getting lost in the messiness of the process and to get to a segmentation framework that is strategically actionable for your business we recommend the following:

- Start by making sure you are clear on the market you are addressing (who is the customer and what problem do we solve)

- Within this market definition develop an understanding of economic needs (we call these alternatively "value elements") relative to your offering and/or your potential offering

- Begin early to develop a value equation based on these economic needs to help determine which of these needs might be most important to your customers and which economic needs your offering can disproportionally address!

- Decide at what level you are segmenting the market. This choice may include direct customers versus end customers or may include companies versus facilities etc. We generally recommend that the right level is related to where there are the biggest differences in value

144

relative to your offering.

- Think through which needs are the best differentiating needs on which to base your segmentation.

- Group your customers with respect to these needs.

- Assess whether these are strategically actionable segments by confirming that

  - Each segment wants a distinct value proposition and all customers with a given segment want essentially the same value proposition.

  - Confirm that the segments defined are identifiable with real customer examples and not simply a hypothetical grouping of needs.

  - Confirm that the segmentation leads to actionable outcomes, including: focus, improved and targeted value propositions and out positioning your competition.

- Conduct VOC to confirm the customer needs, refine and develop the value equation and eventually refine the segmentation as required.

Most Importantly, while we have depicted this process as sequential it is almost always iterative. The segmentation process in B2B markets requires going back and forth between customer economic needs and value we create relative to those needs to arrive at a strategically actionable outcome.

Remove "ity" Words from Your B2B Value Proposition

November 11, 2015 on www.roi-selling.com

When building relationships with buyers, it's important to choose your words carefully. We're not just referring to small talk or the language of negotiation. We're talking about the specific words you use to describe your offering and what differentiates it.

A lot of sellers and marketers make the mistake of using what we call "ity" words when attempting to convey the value of their offering. For example:

- Reliability

- Quality

- Durability

- Flexibility

- Elasticity

- Viscosity

We're not down for these words in general. In fact, depending on who you're talking to, they can be important descriptors. Although the words above might describe your offering, the problem is that they fail to convey the *value* of your offering.

For example, let's say your product increases elasti*city* by five percent. That's a fine statement for your messaging. It describes to engineers and technical experts what your product actually does. But it means almost nothing to the people in charge of giving up a budget to purchase your product. Unless you can describe exactly how that five percent increase in elasticity will advance your customer's business, you're not going to make the sale based on that statement alone.

146

Moving Away from "ity"

The other problem with "ity" words is that they're relative. **Context is everything**. For example, a carpet manufacturer might talk about long-lasting durabil*ity* or high durabil*ity*, which might be true for residential customers; yet in a commercial setting, the carpet might wear out quickly due to the high traffic.

"Ity" words can also be so vague as to become meaningless. For example, for years, Ford's slogan was "Quality is Job 1." But what does that mean? Say you're in India manufacturing cars, and you call them "high qual*ity*" because they last for three years, and that conforms to consumer needs and expectations. If you want to expand to a U.S. market, the claim that you make the "highest quality" cars in India suddenly means something very different, because American consumers have a different expectation about the length of time a car should last.

Similarly, a person buying a Porsche isn't looking for the same definition of quality as a person buying a four-door sedan. In those cases, **quality means different things to different consumers**. To translate product features into value, be specific. For example, does quality mean "lasts longer," "uses the most advanced technologies," or "requires fewer trips to the service garage?"

Conveying Value

Most words that end in "ity" are either so vague or so relative that they fail to usefully convey your value to customers. It's essential to convey to the customer how your product will impact his or her financial statement. Adjectives might describe your product accurately, but for the purposes of your value proposition, you need to push beyond "ity" words. When you come across these words, ask "why?" several times to understand how this adjective conveys to the customer how your **offering will impact his or her business** (https://www.roi-selling.com/blog/focus-on-desired-customer-outcomes-to-improve-revenue-growth).

Again, we wouldn't advise removing "ity" words from your messaging, because if you make a material with a high viscosity, that's something the customer should know. Just remember that you need to be able to push past features and benefits when talking to buyers (and particularly financial buyers) if you want to close the sale.

How to Create a Compelling Value Proposition

January 5, 2016 on www.roi-selling.com

How well can you describe the value of your offering to different market segments? Correctly communicating value at the segment level is critical to any successful business strategy. Unfortunately, many **B2B sales** *(https://www.roi-selling.com/blog/differentiate-yourself-from-the-competition)* and marketing professionals communicate value in broad, generic terms, or fail to customize their language to appeal to different market segments.

To make a successful impact and convey your value effectively, you must be able to articulate how your offering will affect that customer's specific business challenges. I encourage you to start moving away from buzzwords like "state-of-the-art," which is more about you rather than your customer, and generic words like "quality," which mean different things to different people. Instead, start using highly specific words that directly reflect your customer's wants and needs.

Here's an example: Let's say your company makes jet engines. Enabled by some technological advancement, you are able to make the engine more fuel-efficient than anyone else's. Now let's say you have the following target customer groups (segments):

1. Regional airlines

2. Companies with corporate jets

3. Cargo/shipping carriers

Traditionally, sellers and marketers would think about this new jet engine in terms of features and benefits. The feature is the new technology, and the benefit is fuel efficiency. But how would each of the three market segments realize *value* from that benefit? You could go to each of these segments and tout the fact that your engines are more fuel-efficient. But each would probably be left wondering, "I understand that there are fuel savings, but what does that mean to my business?"

Here's a breakdown of how you can illustrate the value of your jet engine in terms that would address the specific needs of each of these segments.

Regional Airlines

Regional carriers generally have a set number of routes and are interested in reducing their fuel cost on those routes. But there also may be some carriers that, by using a highly efficient engine, could fly an extra 100 miles and thus add more city-pairs. That represents a real revenue impact, because they can fly more routes and thus sell more seats.

Value Proposition: A fuel-efficient engine might open opportunities for you to fly to more cities, which would allow you to sell more seats.

Value: Increased revenue with more flights.

Companies with Corporate Jets

Business executives fly on private jets because they want to minimize travel time. And they aren't necessarily going to care about lower fuel costs; they're already spending far more to fly privately than commercially. However, if you can offer business executives a product or solution that allows them to fly faster or farther without having to stop, you've suddenly got their attention. For example, a jet with a more fuel-efficient engine might save them a refueling stop in Anchorage on their way to Beijing. You've saved them time, and their time is worth a lot of money.

Value Proposition: A fuel-efficient engine will shorten your flight duration.

Value: Decreased executive travel time.

Cargo/Shipping Carriers

Cargo airline carriers like FedEx or UPS want to maximize their revenue-per-mile flown. Their need is to fit as many tons of cargo as possible on each flight. A heavier plane has a more limited range and forces carriers to restrict the cargo load to reach all their destinations. Thus, greater fuel efficiency allows the cargo airlines to carry heavier payloads.

Value Proposition:	With a more fuel-efficient engine, you can carry more cargo on each plane.
Value:	Increased revenue per flight.

Market Segments

A segment is a group of customers who have a similar set of needs and thus will value your offering in a similar way. The groups of customers above will all value the benefit of fuel-efficient jet engines in a similar way, but they will all value that benefit differently than the other groups, thus they are different market segments.

Most traditional marketers would simply say, "Our jet engines are more fuel-efficient." But when you stop and look at which factors influence the **buying decision** *(https://www.roi-selling.com/blog/how-are-you-helping-your-buyers-make-confident-buying-decisions)* for each segment, you can start to see where you need to drill down into specifics in order to craft unique messages. As you can see, these are very different ways to talk about value to various market segments, even though all the conversations revolve around the single benefit of a more fuel-efficient engine.

Conclusion

Here are three questions you should consider when creating a value proposition:

1. *What are the unique benefits of our offering?*

2. *Which groups of customers have similar sets of needs that we can address, and can, therefore, become our market segments?*

3. *How will each segment receive value from our offering?*

Section 5: Business Model

Introduction

In our Grassroots Strategy workshops, we tend to get excited about changes in strategy, especially when a creative and insightful segmentation scheme comes together. The risk for us and our clients is that we spend less time than we should thinking about business model. All too often our clients just assume they will deliver the new strategy within the existing business model of the company.

This can prove to be a costly mistake. Strategy ends with value proposition – the promise that you make to customers in a specific segment. But your customers won't pay you for just a promise, you have to deliver outcomes. Business model is the engine that delivers that promise and gets you paid for it, or as one of our clients put it, "business model is your printing press for making profit."

In fact, many of the innovations that have changed our lives over the last couple decades are new business models, not merely products. For example, while the i-pod was enormously successful as a product, Apple's i-tunes ecosystem (which has morphed into the app store) has had far more lasting impact.

So, if you are changing your strategy, rethinking your business model is a must. Do we have all the capabilities required to deliver for the value proposition? Have we figured out a way to execute that is repeatable and scalable? Do we see a path forward to maintain and improve our differentiation such that the strategy is sustainable over time?

As if to reinforce the tendency to underplay business model, there are only a handful of essays in this chapter. But we hope that they are memorable stories and achieve their purpose of encouraging you to think by analogy and fine-tune your business model for lasting success.

Should You Jump on the XaaS Bandwagon?

June 23, 2020

In 1998 Concur revolutionized the software industry by introducing their Software as a Service (SaaS) pricing and delivery model, rather than the traditional license and maintenance model. The model was revolutionary at the time because for a fixed monthly fee, customers got access to a continuous stream of small improvements, rather than getting stuck on an old version and facing a big expense when they chose to upgrade.

Fast forward to today. It is hard to imagine buying most software through anything other than SaaS. Now a recurring theme that we hear from our non-software customers is that they want to move their business to a subscription-based model, but is XaaS (anything as a service) really the best answer for everything?

It turns out that, as is true for most things, XaaS is not the best fit for every offering. There are seven things that need to be true for XaaS to be the optimal answer for your business.

First and foremost, it must be the best answer for the customer!

Sure, a recurring revenue stream with low incremental selling cost sounds great. It makes our financials look great and might even increase our valuation; and it is really alluring to want to be like the "cool kids" in Silicon Valley. But no matter how attractive it looks to your business, XaaS won't work unless it makes sense to the customer. Even in the software world where it frequently is the customer's best option, it took years to convince customers that SaaS was a better model. It not only needs to match how they think about and realize value, but also how they budget and allocate costs.

Your offering must continually deliver more value over time

Even if your offering delivers a lot of value, if the customer could buy it once and forget about it and still receive most or all of that value, it is not a good candidate for XaaS. You need to have a way to continually update and improve the offering in ways that deliver more value to the customer. If either there are limitations to your ability to update the offering for clients or limitations to how you can improve the offering over time, then you probably should consider something other than XaaS.

There needs to be an identifiable/understandable unit of measure

SaaS works because there is a clearly defined and understandable unit of measure for what is being purchased, a user seat. Does such a thing exist for your business? It needs to be something that you can clearly explain to the customer and police over time. It may be possible that you can add something to your offering to, for example, measure and monitor customer usage. But it should be obvious that this needs to be acceptable to the customer and that the cost of monitoring needs to be included in your business case.

XaaS won't create a "perverse incentive" for your customer

This is really important. Make sure that moving to a subscription or XaaS model won't give the customer an incentive to change the way they operate and lower what they pay you. Years ago, we worked with a company that made aircraft brakes. They were trying to undo the damage that had been done when the entire aircraft braking industry had shifted from a price per braking assembly pricing model to a cost-per-aircraft-landing or CPAL (since everything in aerospace needs an acronym) pricing model. The thought was that the brake manufacturers could do a better job of managing the maintenance and life of the brakes. What they missed was that there are two primary ways to stop a plane; brakes or reverse thrusters. The result was that the airline still bore the cost of using reverse thrusters, but the wear on the brakes was no longer their problem. This created a "perverse incentive" for the airlines to encourage pilots to use the brakes more than reverse thrusters, the maintenance cost per landing went up – and this product line's profitability went down.

You must have an easy way to "turn off" your offering

Another reason that SaaS works, is if a customer stops paying, it is easy to disable their access. How would you go about disabling your offering for a customer if they stopped paying? If it requires someone to go to site to disable or remove it, that is problematic.

Your cash flow can support a significant reduction in short-term revenue

This may be obvious, but when you shift from an up-front price to an ongoing subscription, your short-term revenue will often go down. Especially if the new subscription model doesn't dramatically increase customer adoption rates and your offering requires an up-front capital expenditure, your revenue will almost certainly be lower at least for the first year or two. Be sure to take this into account when you are evaluating XaaS as an option.

Your business must have a high fixed cost and low variable cost

Last, but not least, is that your offering must be highly repeatable with very little, or even no, custom work for a new customer. Again, SaaS works because the cost to develop the software is spread across all of the customers and, in general, the cost to add a new customer is low or almost nothing. If your incremental cost to add a new customer is high, it is likely that you will lose money for a significant period of time. The lower your cost to add a new customer, the more suited it may be for an XaaS mode.

Conclusion

An ongoing revenue stream may sound very enticing, but it is not the right answer for every offering. Prices create incentives, and incentives change behavior – be sure to think through all of the implications before making any changes. And, bottom line, even if it sounds good to you, if it isn't the right answer for the customer, as long as they have choices, it will not work.

Is a Semi-Custom Business Model the Right Fit for You?

April 29, 2021

A man in a well-tailored suit will always shine brighter than a guy in an off-the-rack suit. ~Michael Kors

Mr. Kors may be right, there is nothing quite like a real custom-tailored suit. But it has also been one of life's luxuries reserved for the fortunate few – a bespoke suit from one of London's Saville Row tailors will set the owner back at least $2,000 and it could be several times that amount. So, most of us usually settled for an off- the-rack suit, it didn't fit perfectly, but it was a fraction of the cost.

That is until now… in the last several years a new business model allows you to get a made to order suit for about the price of an off-the-rack special. Among the leaders in this space is Indochino – they offer made-to-measure suits, usually for less than $500.

The trick is there is no tailor. You watch a series of on-line videos and have a friend take the measurements (about 20 in all). You then answer a handful of questions about how you like your suit to fit and from there, a model calculates the cutting patterns and sends them off to be produced in Asia. Your new suit arrives about two weeks later (about the time you would wait for the pants to be hemmed on an off-the-rack suit) with exactly the fabric and fit you selected, down to being able to customize the lining or add other detailed touches.

Indochino was started in Vancouver in 2007 by Kyle Vucko and Heikal Gani, former University of Victoria students who disliked their existing clothes-shopping options. Vucko and Gani knew nothing about the clothing business, but they took inspiration from the culture of their tech entrepreneur peers, embracing technology and pivoting quickly to meet customer needs. For example, in 2008, *Men's Flair* posted a less than flattering review of an experience with Indochino. Rather than fight the criticism, Indochino updated their website to address the identified issues and Vucko himself oversaw the adjustments to the reviewer's suit to correct the fit. In a follow up piece, the reviewer credited Indochino with making a 'smart recovery.'

In fact, realizing that when based on self-reported measurements, suits may not be perfect, Indochino started to provide a credit for a local tailor to make it right. In addition, recognizing that some people may not want to take their own measurements, Indochino has opened showrooms where you can not only have a professional take and record your measurements, but you can also touch and feel the fabrics before placing your order.

In truth, even with these improvements, an Indochino suit is not the equal of a bespoke suit – there is no substitute for that second fitting, where the tailor brings a partially constructed suit and checks the drape off your shoulders. On the other hand, for most men an Indochino suit looks way better than off the rack, at a cost that is not much more. And, as they have continued to grow, traditional menswear retailers are feeling the heat. Clearly Covid played a role in the timing, but both Tailored Brands (the parent company of Men's Wearhouse and Joseph A. Bank) and Brooks Brothers (the iconic 200-year-old clothier of the gentry) filed for bankruptcy and announced significant store closings in 2020.

Indochino's success is a great example of what we have come to call the 'ocmi-custom' business model, where a company figures out how to invest upfront to make their product more configurable, thereby providing near custom value at a price that is usually not much more than a standard generic product.

Pulte homes is another example that we have referenced **elsewhere** (https://www.strategy-business.com/article/00180). Pulte figured out years ago how to offer a bounded set of choices for the things that home buyers really want to personalize (e.g., cabinets, counter-tops, light fixtures, etc.) about their homes, while maintaining the scale economies of building largely standard floorplans. Again, the result approximates the value of custom at a price that is little more than standard, and it has allowed Pulte to go from a small regional company building a handful of houses per year in the early 1950's, to a $10 billion+ company in 2020.

So, is a semi-custom business model right for you? Some questions to ask are:

- Is there a repetitive part of your offering that could be automated and/or made more modular? – for example, a design or installation procedure that you do manually, but where most of the process is similar for every job.

- Can you approximate the value of custom with a bounded number of customer choices? – think about the 'turbo tax' interface, where you can answer a limited set of questions phrased in plain English, and the algorithm prepares a draft of your tax return?

- Can you leverage the concept of 'make to order' to drive change in your supply chain? – Dell Computer is a good example of a company that competed on this dimension, revolutionizing the supply chain to turn its inventory nearly twenty times per year (most manufacturing businesses would consider 5-6 turns to be outstanding performance)

- Can you use technology to create a learning engine? – Remember, you don't have to be as good as custom on the first try, there might even be a need for some manual adjustments, but if you are collecting the right feedback data, over time your output will get closer to custom and the manual intervention (and therefore the cost) will go down.

Whether you are building houses, suits, or automobiles, there will always be a market for true custom solutions. This can be a profitable business for the experts who meet these needs, but even the most sought-after tailor still gets paid by the number of hours worked (or by the number of suits). To create a scalable business that can result in a flywheel, you might consider a semi-custom business model. Often this allows you to access a market that is many times bigger than the portion of the market that can afford true custom. You can potentially do this profitably as long as you provide the upfront investment to turn personal expertise into a repeatable process. This requires different thinking, but like a well-fitting suit, the result may be worth it.

Don't Fall in Love with Last Decade's Business Model

June 10, 2021

The Greek myth of Pygmalion, the sculptor who falls in love with the statue he creates, is one of the most enduring stories of all time. The tale shows up in the works of Ovid, the Roman poet who lived in the time of Caesar Augustus. In the 18th and 19th century, the story was dramatically retold by Goethe, Rameau, Donizetti and Gilbert, among others. In the early 20th century, George Bernard Shaw adapted the story for his play, Pygmalion which famously inspired Lerner and Lowe's musical, "My Fair Lady."

Ovid's version of the myth is a story of piety, Pygmalion honors the goddess Aphrodite with prayers and sacrifices and is rewarded by his beautiful statue being brought to life. By the Renaissance the story was mainly interpreted as a cautionary tale of vanity and hubris, only the gods could create perfection, and it was hubris for Pygmalion to believe he could do so himself. George Bernard Shaw uses Pygmalion as a vehicle for social commentary; Professor Higgins gets caught up in his own creation but ignores the real societal issues going on around him and so loses the object of his obsession. While we are not entirely certain of the message of "My Fair Lady," there are some great songs ("I Could Have Danced All Night", "Wouldn't It be Loverly", etc.) and Audrey Hepburn is unforgettable as Eliza Doolittle!

So how is the Pygmalion story relevant to today's business leaders? We have found that often here-to-fore successful organizations fall into what we might call the "Pygmalion Trap". Having had a run of success with a particular market approach or business model, they become convinced that the same approach will continue to be successful into the future. Enamored of their own creation, these business teams often continue to pursue the same historic strategies and practices while ignoring the competitive issues and market changes going on around them, usually to their own detriment.

The story of General Electric over the last 40 years provides a great example of the dangers for a management team who is overconfident in their company's historic strategies and practices and who falsely attributes the reasons for their success. For a long time, General Electric was an admired and iconic company whose history parallels the industrialization of America. The company was formed in 1892 when Thomas Edison merged his Edison General Electric with Thomson-Houston Electric Company. In 1896, GE was one of twelve companies selected for the original Dow Jones Industrial Average and stayed a component of that index longer than any of the others (finally being dropped in 2018). For the next 75-plus years, GE either invented or commercialized everything from refrigerators and televisions to jet engines, literally transforming the way Americans live.

By the time Jack Welch took over GE in 1981, it was a conglomerate with dozens of small, niche businesses. Welch began a massive overhaul of GE's portfolio, famously selling or spinning off a total of 71 businesses that couldn't meet his "be number one or number two" standard. He also acquired companies, some of which, like radio company RCA which owned NBC, took GE farther from its manufacturing roots. By the 1990's, this iconic manufacturing company had become what Welch called a 'boundary-less company,".

In addition to overhauling the portfolio, Welch reinforced a distinct corporate culture that valued training, business and financial management as a discipline and identifying and promoting talent from within. Many at GE believed that their ability to train managers, roll out lean principles and aggressively manage people through force ranking would work in any business. And the results supported this view, with GE going from around $25 billion in revenue to nearly $130 billion during Welch's tenure. Even more impressively, the stock was up over 40-fold from its 1981 level when it peaked in late 2000. Jack Welch had molded GE into a company and a business system whose leadership, as well as many on Wall Street, thought could do no wrong.

However, while GE's performance-based culture had created a generation of leaders who knew how to make their numbers, it was also becoming increasingly internally focused. GE's middle management quickly figured out that the stars got promoted every 18 – 24 months, so they needed to show results in 12 months or less. This led to increasingly aggressive cost-cutting and not nearly enough long-term planning.

Trying to drive long-term initiatives almost exclusively from headquarters, GE made a series of big bets, many of which turned out to be ill-timed or ill-conceived and nearly all of which were poorly executed. Yet they continued to make their numbers. However, if one had bothered to look, the cracks in this great edifice were already showing. A disproportionate share of that growth, and nearly all the excess shareholder returns, were coming from GE Capital, as a series of increasingly aggressive leaders turned the sleepy credit arm that financed appliances and jet engines into the world's largest 'non-bank bank.'

After a highly publicized CEO succession contest featuring Dave Cote, Jim McNerney and others, Jeff Immelt, a consummate GE insider, took the helm in September of 2001, just four days before the 9/11. The financial turmoil and the downturn in aviation that followed September 11 were particularly damaging to GE. Despite the impact on short term results, Immelt was resolute in his belief in the CE system. He maintained the key elements of the business model and culture and continued to diversify away from manufacturing, acquiring 80 percent of Universal Pictures and buying a subprime lender in California. Immelt, GE's management and many on Wall Street remained enamored of Jack Welch's creation but the magic has never returned.

In the financial crisis of 2008/2009 GE Capital was hit with the same liquidity problems that affected all lenders. But since they sometimes operated outside the regulatory frameworks of the banking industry, they were hurt worse. For the most part, the rest of the GE portfolio proved to be anemic, GE management's short-term focus had starved these companies of their long-term growth potential and GE had not put in place a business culture focused on the fundamentals of business strategy and growth. Jeff Immelt left the company earlier than planned in 2017. Jack Welch's creation had lost its luster.

GE is now on its second CEO post-Immelt and has yet to recapture even a hint of the old glory. The tale of its stock price is dramatic: If you put $1,000 into GE stock in January of 2004 (by then the market had recovered most of its 9/11 losses) you would have about $420 today. If you had blindly put that money in the S&P 500, you would have $3,778 today – nearly ten times as much. Oh, and we mentioned Dave Cote, he took over Honeywell in 2002 (after European regulators nixed a planned merger with GE), and by January of 2004 had assembled his team and established his leadership cadence and expectations. $1,000 invested in Honeywell in January 2004 would be worth over $7,500 today!

So, what can we learn from General Electric's fall from grace? Like Pygmalion, it is a story that will be retold and reinterpreted over time, but we believe some lessons are clear:

- Don't assume the business model you have built to succeed in the past will succeed in the future. Make sure to have an objective view of the "Momentum of the business" – how much of your success is being in the right markets vs. gaining share from competitors. Internal focus (we are running ahead of plan!) tends to downplay root causes and underplays the role of luck. We have said it elsewhere, but asking why you are doing well while you are still doing well is one of the most difficult, and most important challenges in business.

- Related to the first point, Strive to be brutally honest about your differentiation – You need to separate the long list of things you are good at to the short list of capabilities that are truly differentiating and for these, to be crystal clear about the source of the differentiation, the evidence that it is real and the way that it provides value for the customer. "We are better managers than the competition" may be true, but it is almost certainly an incomplete (if not misleading) description of your differentiation. And remember, your competition is always evolving.

162

- Teach the basics – rising business leaders need to understand how to think strategically about their markets and organic growth; teaching process improvement and financial principles is not enough. At Honeywell, Dave Cote created a version of GE's famed Crotonville leadership academy, one of the flagship courses was the Strategic Marketing Program, which was eventually delivered to more than 3,000 Honeywell associates attending as part of growth project teams.

- Encourage bottom-up innovation – This is the basic idea behind our book's title, "Grassroots Strategy": more people closer to the customer and the technology thinking of growth and innovation ideas will produce better strategies than relying on big ideas delivered from on high in the ivory tower.

- Establish leadership processes that encourage longer-term, outside-in thinking about the business, trying to avoid the almost inevitable tendency to focus only on 'are you on track to make this quarter?' For example, Dave Cote at Honeywell established 'growth days' where he would do a deep dive with a business unit but structure the meeting around future opportunities explicitly not letting it devolve into an operating review of current year's performance.

- Keep your market understanding current – it sounds obvious, but markets and competitors change. Updating your perspective periodically and objectively assessing the implications is critical. While GE was loaded with smart people, most seemed to believe that as long as they delivered their numbers everything must be ok, causing them to miss lots of warning signs that their market positions were not as secure as they thought.

These are not the only lessons that can be drawn, or even the only way to interpret the story. Books and full-length articles have already been written and more will likely follow. Many of those focus on the personalities and individual foibles of the CEOs, but we believe this gives an incomplete picture. The

163

failings of GE were systemic and symptoms of the same disorders that affect many other companies, internal focus and overconfidence in established management systems. Companies would do well to remember that you can't cost reduce yourself to success and no matter how many quarters in a row you hit your earnings targets, which is no substitute for an informed strategic perspective of your markets and your positions within them.

So, You Want to Be a Software Company?

December 1, 2022

Industrial companies have been trying to evolve to be more like software companies for years. In 2011 General Electric launched GE Digital, and in 2015 Jeff Immelt announced that GE was on track to be a "top 10 software company." Today GE's stock price is 40% of what it was when that statement was made, nowhere near software company valuations. In 2015 Dave Cote stated that he wanted Honeywell to be the "Apple of the industrial sector." In 2016 they launched two software centers of excellence and hired hundreds of people. Honeywell has made some significant changes in their portfolio, and while software plays an increasing role in their offerings, their success in the stock market is due to business performance, NOT a software company valuation.

There is a strong appeal to becoming a software company, but is it really the right answer for your business? As these two examples show, the answer is far from clear.

Why Is it so Appealing?

First and foremost, it is what all the cool kids are doing. Who doesn't want to be Elon Musk and turn a car into a drivable tablet? It harkens back to 1967 when we were told "the future is in plastics," in the movie *The Graduate*.

Next, is the profitability of software. Three of the top ten largest businesses in the US are software companies and five of the most profitable companies are software companies. The gross margins of successful software companies are among the highest around, and making it even more attractive, the software business model is readily scalable. Finally, you have the valuation multiples. Software companies occupy four of the top five companies in market cap valuation. The average multiple of EBITA for a software company is close to double that of the total market average.

The Harsh Reality

The allure of the successful software company masks the reality of the software industry. Low barriers to entry, difficulty differentiating themselves, and the ongoing cost of software maintenance led to some unfortunate results for most software startups.

The failure rate for start-ups is high, and software companies fail at an even higher rate than startups in general. In the first year 20% of startups fail, whereas 50% of software startups fail. After ten years 90% of software companies have failed, while only 70% of all startups fail. Our perception that software companies excel is partly a result of 'survivor bias' – we remember the highflyers and Wall Street darlings, but no one remembers the dozens more that burned out without leaving a noticeable mark on the world.

Some of the reasons software companies fail are the same as any business: They didn't have a clear understanding of the market. They didn't have a clear target segment with a compelling value proposition built on differentiation. The leadership wasn't adequate, often with a product-forward vs. market back perspective. Or they underestimated the fixed cost of creating a marketable software product and ran out of money before they can achieve success.

Key Ingredients of Software Success

Successful software companies are very agile, not just in their software development practices, but in their entire business. They adapt quickly to customer and market requirements. They do not have processes in place that slow innovation. They have an overall vision, but often an incomplete product 'roadmap' – this prevents the 'perfect from being the enemy of the good.'

Most software companies start small and fail fast. They are looking for the Minimum Viable Product and then test new features and capabilities before investing in their complete development. If the market responds positively to the changes, then they rapidly build it out. If the market ignores the new features, then they scrap them and move on.

They also think in terms of total customer lifetime value, rather than just initial selling price. This goes beyond just shifting to a SaaS pricing model, because to retain those SaaS customers, they need to continually deliver more value to those customers. They live the reality of "what have you done for me lately" every day to ensure that they are continually delivering more value.

Lastly, they understand the economics of the software business model. Yes, software is inherently scalable, but the fixed costs can be high as can ongoing maintenance and development costs once you have competition.

Further, costs for customer and technical support are often less scalable, and if not anticipated, can eat you alive.

Can Your Business Be Successful as a Software Business?

There are several attributes that need to be in place to truly shift to a software business.

1) Agile Business Practices – you must either have or be seriously willing to adopt agile business practices. The software lifecycle can't survive hurdles like stage gate reviews.

2) Leadership Philosophy – your senior leadership needs to be nurturing an evolution of success and not looking for the immediate home run. Small successes need to be recognized, but even more so quick failures need to be celebrated. Since software businesses often take years to be profitable, a clear view of leading indicators is usually needed to keep confidence high and investments flowing.

3) Legacy Infrastructure – you must be able to overcome the momentum of legacy infrastructure, such as installed base hardware. If your current business is dependent on a physical product, is the installed base capable of handling the changes required to make changes through software? Or will you need to replace the entire installed base or only sell the new capabilities to new customers?

4) Cashflow Implications – often a shift to a software business model is accompanied with a shift to a more subscription type of pricing model or XaaS.

167

We wrote a post a couple of years ago titled *Should You Jump on the XaaS Bandwagon?* that highlighted some of the requirements to shift to a subscription-based pricing model.

5) Sound Strategy – you still need to maintain a sound strategy. This includes understanding the problems you are solving for target customer segments and how that creates value in a way that you can capture some of that value. The fundamentals of business strategy don't change just because you are a software company. A me-too software product can be just as disastrous as a physical product without differentiation.

Leverage Software

Even if moving to a true software business model isn't right for your company, there are still many things you can do to leverage software and software practices to enhance success. You can migrate your product development practices to be more agile with MVP, rapid testing and feedback, and projects that are measured in weeks, not years.

You can also leverage software to enhance your customer experience. Use digital channels to add more value for end-users. Provide apps, both internally and externally, to automate tedious or knowledge-driven processes. You don't have to be a software company to deliver a best-in-class end-to-end customer experience.

Some B2B companies have even figured out how to incorporate software to change their business models. For example, you might deliver services virtually changing the scalability of product support, or you might use software to dramatically lower the cost of product configuration enabling a semi-custom business model (reference blog).

Conclusion

Although the idea of being recognized as the next Amazon or Apple may be attractive, becoming a software business may not be the right answer for your company. In fact, it could consume disproportionate resources and distract you from more attractive opportunities in your core business.

But adopting software industry practices and philosophies may help your company to be more successful. You should evaluate the best practices and see what applies to your business, but don't throw out the baby with the bathwater because "*the future is in* **software**." Successful companies stay focused on sound strategic principles, continually evolving to create more value for their customers, and their businesses. If software is a piece of that equation, great! But as always, there is no magic bullet and beware of anyone who promises one.

Watt's New? the Product AND the Business Model

June 27, 2024

The first sentence in the U.S. Energy Information Administration's publication, "Electricity Explained" is, "Electricity is measured in units of measure called Watts, named to honor James Watt, the inventor of the steam engine". Once again, we find ourselves having to dispel a myth. The truth is that James Watt did NOT invent the steam engine. In fact, he was late by over half a century. Why then is James Watt so associated with steam power that the internationally accepted unit to measure power is named for him? The answer is that he invented a better product and, more importantly, a better business model.

James Watt was born in Grennock, Scotland. Largely self-taught, he became a metal worker and instrument builder. In 1757, Watt was offered the opportunity to set up a small workshop at the University of Glasgow to maintain and repair its collection of scientific instruments. Fortuitously, in 1763 he was asked to repair a model of a Newcomen steam engine that belonged to the university.

The Newcomen engine was the first commercially successful incarnation of the steam engine. Named for its inventor, Thomas Newcomen, it was a massive device (over 20 feet tall) that used steam power to pump water from underground mines. It had quickly become the standard for large mines throughout Great Britain, but the design had changed little in 50 years, so its use had not extended to other applications.

Upon repairing the model, Watt realized that the design was massively inefficient. Because the entire chamber was reheated with each cycle, more than three-quarters of the incoming energy was wasted as heat rather than being converted to mechanical energy. Watt set about building a better design, and ultimately devised a separate condensing chamber that got around the problem.

While he had the design, Watt had difficulty making it into a commercial product. Specifically, he struggled to find a partner with the capital and expertise to build the new engine at scale. After nearly a decade of frustration and failed ventures, he formed a partnership with Matthew Boulton, who connected him with expert iron workers in Wales.

Boulton's other contribution was the business model. By the 1770's, nearly all large mines already had a Newcomen engine – the de-watering problem had been solved. Owners would need to be convinced that they could save money by replacing the Newcomen engine with the new Boulton and Watt model. In order to speed adoption, Boulton devised a pricing scheme where customers would pay a percentage of the coal saved by the more efficient design. Less coal used to remove water from the mine meant more coal to sell – a straightforward and compelling value proposition.

With the Watt engine quickly becoming the standard in mining, Boulton and Watt started looking for other markets and soon realized that in most other applications the next best alternative was not an inefficient steam engine but rather an even less efficient horse. For example, the horses slowly walking in circles to power hundreds of grinding mills across the British Isles. Adapting their business model, Watt suggested the term 'horsepower' to refer to the number of horses that could be replaced by a steam engine in these new applications. In essence, he reduced the value proposition to one word. Needless to say, the word stuck, it is still how we refer to the power output of an engine.

Lessons for today

This historical tale highlights several key lessons for how companies should think about their strategies:

- First, it is not always about being first to market. Just like Watt did not invent the first steam engine, Sam Walton did not invent the discount store, Michael Dell did not invent the personal computer and Herb Kelleher (Southwest Airlines) did not invent the discount airline. What these founders have in common with Watt and Boulton is that they found a better business model that dramatically improved the value delivered to their customers.

- Second, linking your pricing model to how you create value can help you to sell value and accelerate market penetration. By getting paid directly out of the coal savings, Boulton and Watt both reduced the required capital expenditure and dramatically reduced the risk to new customers ("if the savings aren't real, you don't have to pay"). While this 'guaranteed results' form of pricing is not always the right answer, it is almost always an interesting thought experiment to stretch your thinking about how you could capture more of the value you create.

- Thirdly, by focusing on the problems you solve for customers, you can find ways to expand your potential market. If you have either read **Grassroots Strategy** *(https://www.amazon.com/Grassroots-Strategy-Cultivating-Growth-Ground/dp/0578550067)* or been through one of our workshops you likely remember our market definition 'cube.' Although by the 1780's the Watt engine already dominated the 'small cube' of steam power for mining, they realized that the market for efficient mechanical power was much bigger. Adapting a new business model to sell against horses was a natural extension consistent with their right to win, but they only found it by stepping back and thinking about customer problems, not 'products.'

- Lastly, it is not enough to have the technically best product. It was not until Watt teamed up with Boulton that he had both the resources needed to scale production and the business model required to penetrate the market. Success is almost always a team effort. Your customers pay for outcomes not ideas, so you need **someone skilled in product management** *(https://amphoraconsulting.com/2024/05/31/product-management-holds-the-keys-to-effective-strategic-marketing/)* who can coordinate technology, operations, supply chain and the commercial team to drive results.

Conclusion

Ralph Waldo Emerson famously said, "build a better mousetrap and the world will beat a path to your door" (or maybe he really didn't say it first, but that is a story for another day). But that classic expression only tells half the story. As Watt and Boulton discovered it takes and great product AND the right business model to drive breakthrough growth, and maybe even become a household name. What could this way of thinking mean for your organization?

Section 6: Value Pricing

Introduction

Too often people confuse value pricing with higher prices or planning and executing the next annual price increase. While that is certainly a desirable outcome - higher prices with no loss in volume always looks good in a spreadsheet - the real world is not that simple. Thoughtful value pricing does not necessarily equate to higher prices, instead it means aligning price to value by product and segment.

We often hear clients say that they are good at value pricing because they are commanding a premium. Our next question is usually, ok if you are value pricing, how much of the value that your offering is creating for your customers are you keeping for yourself, vs. sharing with the customer? In other words, could you command even a greater premium? If they don't know the answer to that, then they really aren't value pricing.

These articles explore various aspects of value pricing. They explore the difference between value pricing and other pricing approaches and how value pricing is different from value selling. We also explore the mechanics of value pricing as well as some things to avoid.

We are passionate about helping companies understand the value they deliver to customers and then capturing the optimal share of that value through pricing. We hope that these articles will help you and your organization truly achieve optimal profitability by leveraging value pricing.

You think you know value pricing… and it can still surprise you

October 1, 2019

Our book, "Grassroots Strategy: Cultivating B2B Growth from the Ground Up" has just been published, so driven by some combination of curiosity and vanity, we have been somewhat obsessive about checking our page on Amazon.com. We have been somewhat frustrated that while the book is available to ship in less than a week, Amazon's description says, "usually ships within one to two months." To us, this seems like a great way to scare off potential buyers.

Well, apparently, we are not the only ones who think so. On a recent visit to the site, we noticed that while Amazon lists the new books at our list price of $29.95, there was now an option to purchase a used one for $94.19. That is not a typo, someone is betting that there is a market segment that might pay a threefold premium to get the book earlier.

Grassroots Strategy: Cultivating B2B Growth from the Ground Up

by Jeff W Bennett (Author), Darrin W Fleming (Author)

⭐⭐⭐⭐⭐ ∨   4 ratings

> See all formats and editions

Hardcover
$29.95

1 Used from $94.19
2 New from $29.95

Accelerating profitable growth has been one of the long-standing challenges of business executives. Even today, with stock markets booming and M&A activity returning to record levels, organic growth is anemic for many companies. In our experience, the root cause is a lack of strategy in the organization's thinking, planning, and marketing. Many successful business leaders have built their careers on execution and efficiency but have relatively little experience making the strategic decisions that drive the top line. Lean, Six Sigma, and other efficiency-focused methodologies are fantastic at answering questions around how to do things better, but they are not suited to answer strategic questions around what they should do and why.

‹ Read more

See all 2 images

A little investigation revealed that it is actually a book wholesaler, not just one of our relatives trying to make a buck on a book we gave them. This strange (and probably transient) pricing anomaly helped us realize that it is a good time

175

for a refresher on value pricing.

For starters, what is the goal of pricing? We believe it is to maximize the earnings your company receives... Over the life of the offering... Based on the value it delivers to your customers. Note that this does not say that the goal is to maximize the revenue from each unit you sell this quarter – that is what makes value pricing a challenge, and why it will always be a blend of art and science.

Pricing is a critical component for most companies, but often overlooked or taken for granted (as we did with the price of our book). But it should be a continuous balancing act: if your price is too low you leave money on the table, yet if your price is too high you lose the sale.

The literature is full of case studies on different pricing approaches. While there are probably as many pricing strategies as there are articles on the topic, they can all be grouped into one of 4 categories:

1. Cost-Based Pricing

2. Market-Based Pricing

3. Psychological-Based Pricing

4. Value-Based Pricing

While it may be easier and faster to focus on cost, market or psychological based pricing, it is always best to invest the time and resources into value-based pricing. In our experience, every other pricing approach starts with the wrong reference point. In a B2B setting, the only thing that matters to the customer is how much value they receive when compared to their next best alternative. This sets a maximum price that you can charge, but remember the goal is not to charge the maximum price, but rather the *optimal* price over the life of the offering. That is where the artwork comes in.

Feeling overwhelmed? Here are some key factors to consider when setting your price based on value:

- Competitor response: What are some likely competitor responses? How important is this business to them? Does their cost structure give them flexibility to respond?

- Sustainability: How sustainable and defensible is your differentiation over time? Is your differentiation based on IP or trade secrets that will be difficult to copy, or is it merely assembling available technologies in a way that others could quickly copy?

- Impact on customers' costs: Are you a major expense item for your customers or a small part of their total spending? How do switching costs play into customers' thinking?

- Impact on the broader business: What else do you or can you sell to this customer? What options do they have to shift their business?

Although your maximum price is the incremental value that your offering provides a customer plus the price of their next best alternative, your optimal price needs to take all of these other factors into account. For instance, even if your offering provides a huge amount of value for a customer, if a competitor could quickly replicate your offering, you will need to share a significant amount of that value with the customer. The goal of value pricing is to figure out how much of the total value created you can keep and how much you need to share with the customer in order to maximize the earnings that your company will receive.

So, back to the book: what could the premium seller be thinking? They seem to believe that they offer something unique (guaranteed early delivery) and that this is important to some customers. In addition, they are probably thinking that their scale is infinitesimal compared to Amazon, so a competitor response is unlikely, and since they are selling on-line behind a veil of anonymity, they are probably not too concerned about the impact on sales of other items.

In short, maybe they are not crazy, they might just sell a few, and if not, there is nothing lost. But also, shame on us; it means we may have underpriced. So, buy the book now while it is still a bargain!

177

Value Pricing Relies on Effective Segmentation

December 18, 2019

I was having a conversation with someone the other day about pricing, and it got me thinking about the critical elements of a good value pricing model. Before I get into that though, let me first tell you how our conversation went.

During our discussion on pricing, of course the conversation turned to value pricing (I don't think that I can have a conversation about pricing without it focusing on value pricing). The person said, "I really believe in value pricing. I think that "good, better, best" is a good example of value pricing." My response back to him was that not only am I not a believer in good, better, best pricing, but I don't believe that it is really value pricing at all. That sparked a more spirited discussion.

First, a good, better, best pricing model relies on providing a base-level defeatured version of your product for a low price. A version of your product with all of the bells and whistles at "premium" price. And finally, a mid-range of your product with some, but not all of those features at a price somewhere between the two. At first blush, this could seem like it is pricing to the value of each of those levels. But is it really?

Studies show that in retail, given the option of good, better, best the majority of consumers will choose the better option. Most consumers don't want to be seen as cheap, nor do they want to overspend. Thus, the "better" is often the easiest choice. But does that thought process really translate into the complex buying processes of B2B? With a few exceptions, it does not.

The definition of what is "best" is always in the eyes of the beholder, not what your engineers think, and not what your brochure might say. And too often, 'best' is defined along one dimension (e.g., horsepower or number of settings) and usually fails to capture the complex economic trade-offs that your customers face when deciding what to buy.

In reality, 'best' is defined by each customer based upon their needs. Some customers may have a less complex set of needs based on their situation and therefore the defeatured product adequately solves their problem. That would mean that what we defined as good would really be best for that customer; and worse, what we are calling 'best,' they would call 'over-engineered and over-priced.' Defining different versions of your product as "good, better, or best" is really quite internally focused on what you think, and often almost arbitrary from the customers' perspective. How do you get past that? The answer is segmentation.

Rather than arbitrarily bundling a set of attributes or features, you should first evaluate the needs of your customers. What you are looking for is groups of customers that have the same set of needs, which we would define as a segment. Then you can configure your product to meet those specific needs. When you get done with this exercise, hopefully you will find a handful of different segments where all of the customers have a similar set of needs and you can design product and services to fit the specific needs of each of the segments you choose to target. You may find that the customers that were traditionally buying what you defined as "best" don't really need some of the features that you were providing, and you can lower your cost to serve them without lowering your price. On the other hand, you may find that some of the customers that were buying what you defined as "good" could really use some of the other features, but they weren't willing to pay the price for "best," but by adding those features they would be willing to pay more than you were traditionally charging for "good"

Once you have your target segments and the offerings defined for each, you can then set about value pricing for each segment. By doing this you will likely find that you can both increase your sales to each of the segments and increase your profit margins (by increasing price and/or lowering your costs).

Bottom line, effective value pricing relies on first having a good segmentation that is based on customer needs. Or, as we often say in our workshops, "value and segmentation always go hand in hand." Thoughtfully segmenting your market and understanding the needs of each segment is the only way to fully

179

achieve the benefits of value pricing. For more information on these topics, **Grassroots Strategy** (https://www.amazon.com/gp/product/0578550067) explains segmentation in chapter 6 and value pricing in chapter 8.

Who Should Own Pricing in Your Organization?

April 3, 2020

Don't Make These Mistakes When it Comes to Pricing

Pricing is one of the most important levers your organization has, therefore pricing decisions are some of the most important it will make. Set the price too high, and you won't sell anything. Worse yet, set the price too low and you are leaving money on the table.

That leads to the question, what department or function within your organization is in the best position to set the price in order to maximize earnings? Over the years, we have heard a lot of strong opinions. Some (usually salespeople) say that since sales is closest to customers that they should be in charge of price. Others believe that operations or finance should control prices because they have the best understanding of the cost of the offering. We have even seen companies establish an independent pricing group that reports outside the day-to- day operations, in one case, even reporting to legal!

We are going to make the case that pricing should almost always be owned by strategic marketing.

Why Shouldn't Sales Own Pricing?

Although sales have more actual interaction with customers and are likely to have first-hand knowledge of competitive offerings and prices in their area, there are several reasons that sales should not have ultimate price authority. That is not to say that sales shouldn't be given some price discretion, within a set of bounds, but that the price framework and the discounting rules should be maintained elsewhere.

A big reason, but not necessarily the most important reason, is that historically most salespeople are compensated based on sales revenue. Knowing that lower prices can 1) attract more customers and 2) help overcome customer objections, sales has a natural incentive to lower prices. Even if a company has made a shift to compensating sales on margin or profitability, salespeople

181

will tend to price too low. This is due to a built-in asymmetry in incentives: price too low, and they get a slightly lower commission, price too high and they get nothing. But incentives aside, there is an additional problem with sales owning pricing.

Salespeople only have insight into their target customers or what's happening in their particular territory or region. What is true for them does not necessarily hold true for other markets, other territories, or the competitive situations of their colleagues. As mentioned earlier, sales should often be allowed some price discretion so they can respond to local market conditions. But that leeway should be limited, because individual pricing decisions can sub-optimize pricing on the aggregate, which can damage overall profitability for the company.

What Happens if Operations or Finance Own Pricing?

The primary point of reference for both operations and finance is cost. This inherently leads to the price being set based on CoGS, or at best the total cost to serve. As we have discussed before, price should always be based on value and not based on cost.

True, cost is one input to pricing – specifically, you should never price below your cost because you can't make it up in volume. But pricing based on target margins over cost is using an internal reference point that is completely unrelated to customer value.

Sometimes organizations will use external sources and 3rd parties to evaluate competitive pricing in the market and set prices based on those sources. Although this market-based pricing is one step better than cost-based pricing, it still doesn't take into account differentiation and value delivered. Often, relying on pricing gurus is putting a band-aid on the underlying issue – no one else can be trusted to set prices because they lack the information, tools or incentives.

Why Marketing Should Own Pricing?

Strategic marketing is about understanding customer needs and value at each step in the value chain and using this understanding to build and maintain differentiation that allows us to capture more value in our target segments. Pricing to maximize earnings over the life of an offering is an integral part of this function. An effective strategic marketing team should have all the elements to set the price based on value:

- Market understanding of customer needs

- The customer's next best alternative (think competitors)

- Your offering's differentiation relative to that next best alternative

- The value created by that differentiation.

- Groups of customers that have similar sets of needs (segments)

- The total cost to serve each segment of customers

- The potential impact that the price of this offering could have on other offerings.

Marketing, when done properly, is in the best position to set the optimal price for each segment of customers. Obviously, they shouldn't do this in a vacuum. They should rely on input from sales, operations, and finance to ensure that they have the most accurate picture of the situation, but marketing should almost always be the owner of pricing.

Summary

Setting your optimal price means that you are maximizing the total lifetime profitability for the offering. That means you have delivered adequate value to your customer while capturing enough value to be profitable and continue to invest. But importantly, it does not mean maximizing price on each individual transaction.

We find that, all too often, when someone other than marketing owns pricing, it is a sign that there is a gap in strategic marketing capabilities. If your marketing team is consumed with the activities of marketing and not driving pricing decisions, it may be time to invest in building a strategic marketing capability. In the words of one of our customers, "marketing is more than marketing."

How Does Inflation Impact the Value You Deliver?

October 4, 2022

Inflation is hitting every sector of the economy, and almost every company we talk to is grappling with raising prices to compensate for their rising costs. Invariably someone will say, "Raising prices is value pricing, right?" Our answer is, not really. Although value pricing could lead to an increase in price, it could also lead to holding price or even lowering price.

Value pricing is always relative to your customers' next best alternative (NBA). During inflationary times your customers' alternatives are likely impacted by inflation, but the impact could be very different. Value pricing in inflationary times, then, is reassessing your price against the current value of your customers' alternatives.

So, there are two key questions. How does inflation impact the value you deliver? And how do you best implement the revised pricing?

Value Pricing Review

Before we answer these questions, let's review the basics of value pricing. The maximum price you can charge is the price of your customer's NBA plus (or minus) the incremental value your customer will receive from your offering relative to that alternative. The value equation provides your maximum price.

$$\text{Price} <= \text{Price(NBA)} + (\text{Value(you deliver)} - \text{Value(NBA)})$$

We always stress that it is important not to limit your thinking on the customer's NBA. Directly competitive products are certainly alternatives, but so are substitutes for your offering such as alternative materials, formulations, technologies, etc. You also need to consider the customers' ability to use less of your offering, or not use it at all. For example, when fertilizer prices are higher (all else being equal), farmers will use less fertilizer.

185

How does inflation impact your ability to value price?

All of your customer's alternatives can move in times of inflation, so it's important to reassess your value. Directly competitive products likely have similar economics and will move in highly correlated ways. But substitutes may move in markedly different ways in magnitude and potentially even direction.

This reminds me of my freshman college economics class, and the importance of evaluating all tradeoffs. The story my professor told was on the tradeoff between choices of alcoholic beverages (obviously he was playing to his audience). If the price of beer were to go up because of a shortage of hops, then some beer drinkers may change from choosing between different brands of beer, to buying a different form of alcohol altogether, like gin. I am fine with either beer or gin, so I am not sure it is much of a tradeoff. Can your customers switch to alternative ways to meet their underlying needs if you raise prices too much?

So where do the increases in your cost show up in the value equation? THEY DON'T. Your cost is never part of the value equation. Seeing cost increases due to inflation is simply a signal that marketplace costs, and likely product values, are changing and that it may be time to revisit your pricing. Cost and margin should only surface when deciding whether the returns are sufficient to continue participating in this business.

For consideration: If raising prices because of raw material inflation is NOT value pricing, why does it persist? Four hypotheses:

- It usually works (1) – competitors likely have similar cost pressures and so the price of the next best alternative is (or will) likely go up as well.

- It usually works (2) – almost everything is inelastic in the short-term, so small changes in price will likely not result in customer completely re-evaluating their supplier decisions, especially when their business faces other pressing problems (like supply chain issues and trying to raise prices to their customers)

- It is inwardly focused – like all cost-based pricing, it starts with the internal perspective that we need to maintain margins or still hit our financial goals… but like all cost-based pricing that makes it easy, but doesn't make it right (see previous blog on why cost-based pricing persists)

- It is easy to sell – being able to point to raw material price increases often gives a sales force the extra courage to implement a price increase and not discount away the gains.

How do you best implement revised pricing?

Make no mistake, we support raising pricing when you can – when your price goes up and volume stays the same, it always looks good in a spreadsheet (and on your bottom line). That doesn't mean that it will work that way in the real world. Our experience is that how you implement a price increase plays a big role in its impact, both short-term and long-term.

Broadly speaking, there are three mechanisms for managing pricing in inflationary times: simply revising all-in prices, indexing prices, or adding a surcharge separate from the price. Each has its place.

Revised all-in prices are most appropriate when the impacts of inflation are smaller and/or less volatile, and when your relative value moves in more complex ways vs competitors and substitutes. A benefit of this approach is that it naturally keeps the focus on value.

Indexed pricing is most natural when one or a few key inputs (raw materials, feedstocks, additives) account for the majority of the product value and when indices for those few inputs are easily established. A significant drawback of indexed pricing is that the indices do not account for any changes in relative value; it's possible that indices on autopilot could drive your price too high relative to your value resulting in lost volume or could leave your price too low vs alternatives (resulting in lost value capture). And while it is possible to maintain a value price with indexed pricing, another drawback is that it naturally tends to shift the focus to cost.

Surcharges work well when inflation impacts are significant and more volatile and when indexed pricing is not preferred. Surcharges provide good transparency for the inflationary elements while preserving a separate value price, and they are sometimes easier to sell when they impact something that is already a separate line item, like freight. The same drawback as noted with indexed pricing applies here with surcharges; leaving surcharges on autopilot can result in over-pricing (lost volume) or underpricing (lost value capture).

What are the common pitfalls in value pricing during inflationary times?

In addition to understanding the mechanisms for implementing price changes related to inflation, effectively implementing value pricing updates means guarding against some common pitfalls.

1. Focusing too narrowly on competitive pricing and/or inflationary costs

During inflationary times, what previously may not have been a realistic alternative (e.g. substitute) may have become your customer's best option, changing the NBA benchmark price and your incremental value. It's critical to keep your eye on your direct competitors AND on the broader set of alternatives. Not detecting your customers' ability to substitute would lead to mistakenly high prices.

There is a flipside as well. It can be the case that inflation has put more distance between you and substitutes by increasing the incremental value of your offering. In this case, if you are a price leader, there is an opportunity to lead pricing north. Again, this hinges on an understanding of value broadly across both direct competitors and other alternatives/substitutes.

2. Failing to make prices stick

Remember, the value equation only gives you the maximum price you can charge. Even if you know this quantity exactly, there is some artwork in how much you can capture. As you try to deploy value pricing, the market and even your own organization can conspire against you. When roll out new pricing, it is important to consider the extent to which inflation has changed the factors that determined how much of the value you can capture, especially competitor pricing behavior and your ongoing ability to differentiate.

It's also critically important to ensure that your own company's behavior doesn't limit the ability to capture the new value price. The most common culprit is discounting. As an example, a client who did a great job of properly assessing and setting value price captured very little of that price because the sales force was incented on total dollars of sales and had latitude to discount. Adding insult to injury was the quarter-end push for revenue that also drove incremental freight and handling costs on top of the discount.

3. Improperly communicating reasons for price change

When updating prices to address inflationary impacts, it's important to convey that the price changes are based on value economics (not whimsical) while not giving away any cost information that could be used against you. The approach to communicating will vary depending on the mechanism used.

With an all-in price change, communication should focus on how inflation impacts the differential value vs. competitors and substitutes. It can and should touch on specific inflationary drivers and how inflation impacts the value of those alternatives. It should also avoid tight linkage to specific inflationary cost impacts for your products. If inflationary impacts are very similar for you and your competitors, then emphasizing competitive price movement can help avoid the cost focus.

With index pricing and surcharges, the inflationary drivers are laid bare. Using published indices helps to avoid disclosure of any costing. When customers desire to validate modeling (i.e. by translating indices to surcharges based on composition of product impacted by inflationary drivers), it's possible to validate without disclosure by using third party auditing.

4. Inadvertently setting up longer term price reductions

Setting up unintended longer-term price reductions can be an issue with any of the pricing mechanisms but is more often an issue with indexed prices and surcharges. Setting the expectation that your price is tied to some index necessarily means that when that index comes down your price will come down as well. Be sure to test the limits of the index to assess the range of outcomes.

Even with this diligence, you still may need to reduce price over time. If your relative value drops because competitors strengthen their offerings, it will be necessary to reduce your prices. But this is an action based on value change and is not a mistake in your framework or modeling.

5. Creating perverse incentives

No matter what your intentions are with pricing, your customers and the market will always act in their own best interest. It is far too easy to unintentionally set up a system that allows customers to game it to your disadvantage.

An example of this is a client that made packaging film from petroleum-based material. During the spike in oil prices in 2008, they implemented an oil surcharge that was updated quarterly. In the fall of 2008, the price of oil fell from a peak of $140 per barrel to around $60 within a quarter. In Q4, their customers knew that their price would drop significantly beginning in Q1, so rationally, they delayed their orders – the company went nearly six weeks without a single new order!

That alone is bad enough, but the situation was exacerbated because their product was usually made to order. Their high capital cost meant that the client kept their production lines running and so they produced stock based on their best guesses of thickness, width, etc. Unfortunately, their best guesses didn't match the slew of orders that arrived in Q1 when the prices dropped. They were immediately behind in fulfilling the new orders and took nearly a year to work through the mismatched inventory they had accumulated.

Summary

In the end, it's important to remember what we call the "iron law of the marketplace:" customers will not pay more than the value they receive. Period. And the value customers receive has nothing to do with your cost to deliver your offering. Inflation doesn't change that fact, but inflation can have significant, even disruptive effects, on the economics of the customer's alternatives. So, periods of inflation should trigger reevaluation of the cost economics of your customer.

Raising prices just because your costs have gone up is still cost-based pricing. But if prices are going up for other alternatives, this may present opportunities, and if you haven't done so for a while, it may be a great time to re- ground your understanding of what value really means to your customers.

5 Pitfalls to Avoid when Value Pricing Software

April 19, 2023

We had a client many years ago that was struggling with how to bring a new software offering to market, specifically how to price it. Their core product was equipment used in manufacturing processes and the associated parts and accessories. The equipment was a large capital purchase for their customers, but they made most of their money from the ongoing purchase of parts and accessories (think razor blades). Their new software would help their customers design and optimize their manufacturing process and choose the best mix of parts and accessories. The challenge lay in the fact that, although the software would create tremendous value for their customers, it had the unfortunate side effect of frequently reducing the number of parts and accessories that they needed to buy. The leadership team was stuck with some wanting to postpone the software release indefinitely and others wanting to price it very high to make up for the potential lost parts revenue – and no one really thinking about customer value.

Software pricing can be complicated and confusing, but it need not be a reason to panic – even for organizations that are more comfortable pricing hardware. The primary thing to keep in mind is that all the rules of customer value still apply. Below are several of the pitfalls that we see customers fall into when pricing software, and some thoughts on how to avoid them.

Pitfall: Not being able to measure value

Too many software packages over-promise and under-deliver – think ERP implementations. As a result, most customers are skeptical of software-based solutions where they have not used them before. To overcome this, you should strive to measure value in a way that is believable and demonstrable. In this case, our client got it right. They gave away 50 beta versions of the software and compared the results at those plants to 50 matched plants that continued current practices. This gave them an accurate and credible way to estimate the value for future customers (and gave them critical insight into how and where to improve the software).

Remedy: Strive for an independent and objective way to measure value, do not assume the customer will accept 'trust me' as evidence

Pitfall: Using the wrong reference point to measure value

It is critical that you understand the reference point of value from the customer's perspective, which is their next best alternative. In the case of the equipment manufacturer, they had been thinking that they needed to price the software to overcome the reduction in sales of parts and accessories. That was an internal reference, not a customer reference. While it was true that the customer would see value in the reduction of those costs, the bigger value was in the optimization of their manufacturing process (e.g. less downtime, higher throughput, etc.).

Remedy: Always start with the next best alternative (from the customer's perspective, not yours, when measuring value.

Pitfall: Failing to anticipate the next best alternative

The software world moves quickly, with start-ups and spin-offs launching new products all the time. For this reason, it is even more critical to anticipate what the customer's next best alternative might be, not just what they do today. In this case, if our client failed to release the software to extend machine life, it is likely that someone else eventually would. Remember: if there is a better way to solve a customer's problem, someone will find it.

Your job is to make sure that someone is you!

Remedy: Think broadly about next best alternatives and honestly ask "how hard would it be for someone else to do this?"

Pitfall: Ignoring the drivers of value

Another important factor to consider when pricing software is the source of the value, and more specifically one or two metrics that correlate to value in such a way that you can use them to set your price. The equipment manufacturer came in thinking that they were going to price their software based on a seat license per user.

Although that is a very common way of pricing software, the number of users had very little correlation with the value that the customer could receive. A single user could be using the software to optimize anywhere between 1 and 50 pieces of equipment or production lines. The metric that mattered was the number of production lines.

Remedy: Dig deep to understand the underlying source of the value and identify a metric that correlates with that value when choosing what metric drives your price.

Pitfall: Not linking price to the goals of the business

We typically say that the goal of value pricing is to optimize the earnings impact on the business. If your goal as a business is to grow a profitable, self-sustaining business, then that statement is absolutely true. Although with software, too many companies get it wrong.

Not that long ago, it was common for companies to give away software to sell more hardware, because selling more hardware had always been the business goal. While this may have been historically true, it is clearly short- sighted. Over time it generally gets harder to differentiate on hardware alone, but software and analytics become more important – a balanced pricing approach that aligns price with where the long-term value is created is more likely to succeed.

In the pure software world, many smaller companies have a different goal: to maximize the valuation of the business for an equity event (sale or IPO). Valuation is often driven by metrics such as growth in subscribers, low customer churn, and/or growth in Annual or Monthly Recurring Revenue (ARR). The fundamentals of value still apply, but the decision on pricing to that value is often driven to optimize those metrics rather than purely profitability. In the end though, there still needs to be a path to profitability. Smart investors will look at the whole package, and if there is not a path to sustainable profit, they will stay away no matter how good one of these metrics may appear.

194

As an example, one of our clients had a goal of having a million users of their software, so they literally gave it away. Even so, only about 50 percent of customers ever used the software and those who used it never relied on it for a regular part of their business. As of this writing, they hit their goal of a million users but are still struggling to create ANY revenue from the software offering.

Remedy: Start by confirming what you are trying to achieve as a business and have a clear and aligned set of expectations and goals for your software that are linked to long-term value creation.

Pitfall: Overcomplicating pricing

Because software is so configurable, it is far too easy to overcomplicate your pricing. You can have different levels (e.g. free, standard, pro), different modules, different add-ins, etc. While that flexibility can provide you the power to price-differentiate for customers who can self-select what they need (their segment), it also gives them the ability manipulate your pricing in their own best interest (as they should). Trying to "trick the customer" into buying something they don't need usually ends poorly. In the case of the equipment manufacturer, their simplest and best pricing metric was based on the number of pieces of equipment being managed

Remedy: Start with the simplest pricing model that you can construct that links to the driver(s) of value. You can always expand it over time (if expanding looks like it will deliver value over your first, simple approach).

Pitfall: Using the wrong business model

Some of the biggest business innovations over our lifetime have been business model innovations. Launching a new software offering provides a great opportunity to introduce, or at least explore, a new business model. Don't get stuck in the mode of thinking business as usual.

In the case of the equipment manufacturer, they were initially thinking about per seat software license that was priced to try to overcome the anticipated lost sales in parts and accessories. What they launched was a price per piece of equipment model that had a built-in capability to directly place the order for the required parts and accessories per the design. What they achieved was a closer connection with their customers and increased sales for two reasons. First, it was easier for customers to order, and they had higher confidence in ordering the right part for their specific configuration. This slowed the penetration of third-party parts and accessories. Second, and even more importantly, as the software-enabled ordering and tracking of parts became embedded in customers' way of doing business, it helped our client in securing additional equipment sales.

Remedy: When launching a new software offering, step back and consider multiple business models, then pick the business model that both delivers the greatest life-cycle value to the customer and that allows you to capture the largest share of that value.

Conclusion

Although there are many pitfalls to avoid when setting your pricing strategy for a new software offering, but it is important to remember that the fundamental rules of customer value still apply. Taking time to evaluate your business goals for the software, value drivers, pricing structure, and business model options can help to avoid these traps and deliver improved business performance.

Five Requirements to Being a
Value Pricing Champion

August 28, 2023

Value pricing is an elusive topic but when done properly it can lead to long periods of exceptional profitability. We often hear companies improperly refer to their pricing methods as "value pricing," when they are far from it. Like anything else, just using the words does not improve results, you actually have to use the framework to make different decisions about pricing. And because the competitive landscape changes over time, your value pricing needs to evolve over time. There are some things that you can do to ensure that your value pricing strategy will deliver the desired results.

Pricing Schemes Masquerading as Value Pricing

Value pricing starts with understanding the differential value your offering delivers to a customer relative to their next best alternative. There are several pricing schemes that may appear to be value pricing but are not. Here are a few examples:

- Premium pricing: although this may appear to be value pricing, unless you set the premium based on measurable customer value then you are merely guessing at what the price should be. Not value pricing.

- Raising prices: if you raise your prices and don't lose customers that would seem to indicate that you are delivering customer value relative to their next best alternative, but if you don't understand the differential value your offering delivers relative to their next best alternative then you are merely guessing (and lucky if you don't lose customers). Not value pricing.

- Pricing to total value created relative to doing nothing: unless there truly isn't another competitive alternative, pricing to the total value your offering creates is problematic. It ignores the possibility that another alternative could deliver some of that value and risks losing the customer to a competitor. Value pricing misunderstood.

197

- Tiered or package pricing: if the tiers are designed for specific segments of customers with specific needs that are met by a specific grouping of features and delivers a specific amount of value then this could be value pricing. That is rarely the case though, it is often just bundling to get higher prices or worse yet volume discounts. Not necessarily value pricing.

Most pricing schemes are poor substitutes for true value pricing but are often used because they are easier. Don't be lazy. Do the hard work to implement value pricing if you want to see results.

Two Examples of Value Pricing Failure Modes

Example 1: Not Understanding Value by Segment

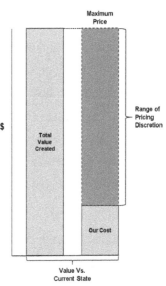

In this example the company was pricing their product relative to the next best alternative of the majority of the market. Because for the majority of the market their product didn't deliver any additional value relative to an entrenched competitor, they were discounting their product, not just a little bit, but up to 80% off the price of the predominant alternative. In the end it turned out that for a specific segment (about 15% of the total market), specific features of their offering delivered value of 2-3 times the price of the competitive offering. By pricing to value in that segment of customers, and not trying to compete where they could not win, they were able to raise their prices by a factor of 8 (not 8% but 800%), lower their selling cost and dramatically improve their profitability.

Example 2: Pricing against Current State rather than Alternative Solutions

In this example the company was trying to price to the total value created by the solution relative to what their customers were doing today. Unfortunately for them, there were other competing solutions in the market that delivered most of the value that their offering created and were priced significantly lower.

198

This meant that they were closing very few sales at their intended price and the handful of uninformed customers who did buy experienced serious remorse when they discovered that there were competing alternatives. With sales lagging well behind plan, the company changed their strategy to focus on specific solution areas where the competing alternatives did not work as well. This allowed them to capture more value as well as lower their cost to serve.

Value Relative to Do Nothing

We are often faced with situations in which we are selling to potential customers where we can clearly see that our solution will create value (for example save the customer money) relative to what they are doing today. In these instances, we may be tempted to believe that we can price to this customer or other similar customers in the market relative to the "total value created" (see right). In reality, "total value," although enticing, is usually irrelevant – value is by definition always relative to the next best alternative. Yes, with some new to the world products, there is no existing in-kind solution, and in these rare cases, you can value price relative to the 'do nothing' alternative or status quo solution. However, if alternatives similar to your solution exist or could be developed quickly then pricing to capture all of this a value would be a misapplication of value pricing.

However, if alternatives similar to your solution exist or could be developed quickly then pricing to capture all of this a value would be a misapplication of value pricing.

Value Pricing Relative to a Competitive Alternative

In general, a competitive alternative either exists, or could exist in the near future, which delivers at least some of the value that your offering creates. So, your maximum price is actually limited by the competitor's price and the differential value that your offering delivers relative to that competitive alternative.

Don't be fooled by the total value created when a competitive alternative exists (or could easily exist in a very short time). Although this does provide value for the customer, you cannot price to that total value and win – customers are smart enough to find alternatives, even if they are not currently aware of them. Some of our clients

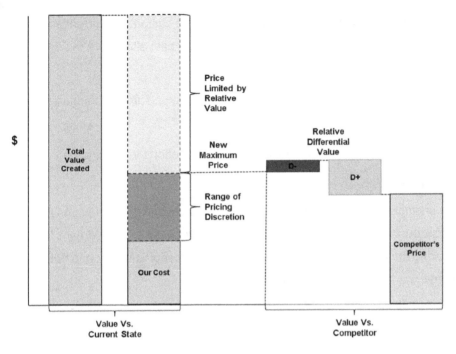

have lamented that this means prices are determined by the 'dumbest competitor,' and there is some truth in this. If all similar solutions were priced relative to the old status quo, prices would be higher for everyone. However, short of collusion (illegal, at least in the US), there is no way to force this outcome – good marketing strategies have to work in the world as it is, not the world as we wish it to be.

Five Musts to Value Pricing

There are a few imperatives to improve your value pricing.

1. Understand the value your offering creates for the customer relative to the current state.

2. More importantly understand the value your offering creates relative to the current next best alternative.

3. Make sure you understand where further competitive alternatives could come from and when they are likely to be available and how this will change the relative value you create.

4. Make sure your price is set not just based on the customer's current state, but on their next best alternative or their likely next best alternative in the near future.

5. Frequently evaluate the competitive landscape to be sure that things haven't changed.

Missing just one of these steps will undermine your efforts to value price.

Conclusion

Value pricing, when done right, is one of the quintessential mechanisms to optimize business profitability. But doing it well requires a commitment to embracing the concepts, using them correctly, and keeping them up to date as markets and competitors evolve.

Does Strategic Pricing Stop Value Leakage to Optimize Profits?

November 30, 2023

Many times, when we talk to clients about pricing, they say that they have already worked out pricing because consultant XYZ did a strategic pricing initiative for them. As we ask questions about what they actually did, we usually uncover that the initiative was really more of a transactional pricing analysis, which for some reason is often called "strategic pricing."

In our view, real strategic pricing always starts with a clear understanding of the value you create for customers and how this is different from their alternatives. In our water pipe analogy for value leakage, this is the input – the water pressure at the source, if you will. Fixing leaks in the pipe is great, but you can never get more than what you started with, which is why we are so adamant about the starting point being the customer value that you create.

That is why we find it very ironic that the most tactical part of pricing is what is often referred to as "strategic pricing." We would call transactional pricing Price Discipline, and it is the one place in our value pricing framework where value isn't really taken into account. This is the final step where you are attempting to eke out the last couple of percent of price. While it is the last in our framework, it is where many companies start their pricing efforts, so let's explore it a bit deeper.

Price Discipline

The first, and often easiest area to stop value leakage is ensuring that you have price discipline within your organization. Is your sales team unnecessarily discounting, or giving customers volume discounts even when the volume commitments weren't hit? Are you providing warranty or other service beyond what is necessary?

Now we have done our share of transactional pricing work, and the results are almost always positive. Even though these efforts are not necessarily grounded in customer value, there are several reasons why they work:

- Companies are often reluctant to raise prices and may need a push to motivate them. We have to laugh when we hear "we raised prices and didn't lose a customer" – this doesn't mean you are now value pricing, it just means that your prices are probably still too low!

- Nearly everything is price inelastic in the short term – raising prices 2-3 percent is rarely enough to get your customers to search for alternatives, especially if you are not a major component of their cost structure. However, this too is not value pricing and may backfire in the long run when your customers do evaluate their options.

- Pricing and discount structures tend to get more complicated over time and almost certainly contain anomalies – we remember one client where we discovered that average discounts across regions were correlated with the average tenure of the sales rep – yes, the longer a rep had been in a region, the lower their relative prices.

So, while good transactional pricing analysis almost always produces some short-term gains, it is not a substitute for value pricing. Value pricing is always grounded in the economic value of your offering to the customer. This requires a clear understanding of your differentiation and an objective perspective on how customers value that difference. Nor is price discipline the only type of value leakage. Let's explore the other areas of value leakage from continuing to work from right to left.

Value Selling

Imagine walking into a Mercedes dealership to buy a car. You look at different models, test drive one or two, and evaluate available options. After deciding which model and specific features you're interested in, the sales rep comes back with a price.

At this point, you pull out a Hyundai ad and tell the rep you can go down the street and get this car for half the price. Do you think the dealership will negotiate with you on price? Absolutely not! They will tell you to go talk to the Hyundai dealer. Why? Because they know that the next best alternative for their target customers is not Hyundai, and that you are wasting their time.

In B2B sales, understanding your differentiation and demonstrating how that creates value for your target customers is crucial. This requires clear segmentation communicated to your sales team and often value selling tools to help them highlight the value created to prospective customers and prevent them from falling back into bad habits like negotiating against the wrong alternative.

Value Sharing

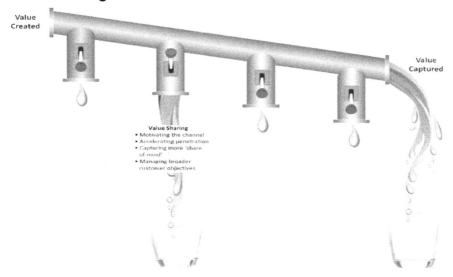

This brings us to the only area of value leakage that is necessary. In order to motivate your customer, you must share some of the value you create. Value sharing may also be required with channel partners along the value chain. The amount of value that you share vs. the amount that you capture is the art of value pricing. We explore value pricing in many other posts and aren't going to go deeper here. It requires long-term insights into both customers and competitors to anticipate their range of responses.

Value Understanding

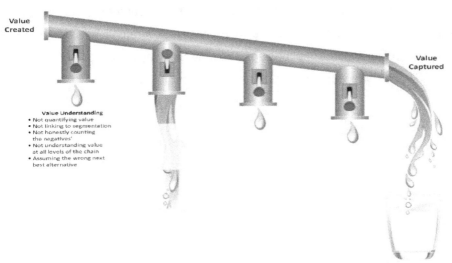

Value
Created

Value
Captured

Value Understanding
- Not quantifying value
- Not linking to segmentation
- Not honestly counting
  the negatives'
- Not understanding value
  at all levels of the chain
- Assuming the wrong next
  best alternative

This is usually the biggest leakage point because it is the most difficult to overcome. In fact, it is more like

untapped pools of water that never make it into the pipe in the first place. As we've said elsewhere, developing an informed understanding of customer value requires deep insight into your customers, or as we like to say, "becoming a student of your customer." Also, since value is always relative to the customer's next best alternative, you must also have a deep and realistic understanding of the competitive alternatives. If you don't know how much value you create, you can't hope to capture any of it.

Conclusion

Remember, your ultimate goal is value capture. The only way to optimize your value capture is to first stop the value leakage by not understanding value, not selling the value you create, and not maintaining price discipline.

What is often referred to as strategic pricing is really more focused on enforcing pricing discipline through an analysis of transactional pricing. Although this analysis can deliver some significant bottom-line results, it is not likely to fix all of the areas you are leaking value. You need to start with a strong understanding of the value your offering creates, price to that value, and train your sales team to sell based on that value to optimize your total value capture. We are on a mission to stamp out the improper use of "strategic pricing" when really referring to transactional pricing. The only real way to stop price leakage is Value Pricing, which is therefore the only real Strategic Pricing!

The Important Distinctions Between
Value Pricing and Value Selling

February 21, 2023

I recently reflected on what might cause sellers to reassess their value pricing and value selling strategies in a changing economy. While both are rooted in value, value pricing and value selling use different tools with different purposes and reference sets. Let's take a moment to review the basics.

Value Pricing Fundamentals

Value pricing considers all relevant factors and is the best way to optimize your business performance through price. You begin by understanding the value your offering creates for a customer.

Keep in mind though that value must be considered relative to the customer's next best alternative (think competitor) when evaluating your price. Since you can't charge a premium for something your competitor can do just as well, you must understand the incremental value your offering creates for the customer. This competitor or market price is the starting point for your value pricing equation.

Your maximum price is the price of the customer's next best alternative (again, think competitor) plus the incremental value your offering delivers relative to that alternative. This then sets the upper limit to your price.

Your cost sets the lower limit—not to calculate your price, but to ensure that your price is greater than your cost. You now have the upper and lower limits of your pricing.

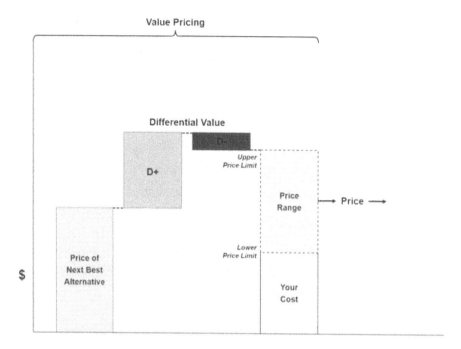

Value Pricing

Differential Value

Here is where the nuance comes in. The key to value pricing is choosing the earnings optimizing price within those limits. You need to share at least some of that value with the customer, but obviously you want to keep as much as possible for your business. You can read more about this value pricing dynamic **here** *(https://www.roi-selling.com/blog/how-to-price-your-solution-using-value-pricing).*

The key thing to note is that the price of the next best alternative is a significant reference point when setting your value price.

Value Selling Fundamentals

Value selling focuses on *justifying* your price, not *setting* your price. Justifying your price uses metrics such as Return on Investment (ROI) and Net Present Value (NPV). These metrics estimate whether the customer's business is better or worse off by investing in your offering, relative to what they are doing today, NOT relative to the competitor.

There may be the rare occasion where the customer wants to get into a **Total Cost of Ownership (TCO)** *(https://www.roi-selling.com/blog/comparing-roi-and-*

tco-which-is-better-to-win-more-deals) analysis to compare your offering against a competitor. That doesn't justify the investment, it only analyzes the total lifecycle cost between the two alternatives. The good news is that if you have done Value Pricing properly, you will win on a TCO analysis as well.

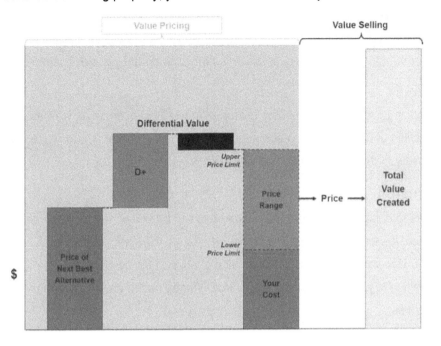

Implications

Although value pricing and value selling both rely on the value you create, their primary difference is their respective reference points.

- Value pricing uses your competitor's price as a reference point.

- Value selling uses your customer's current state as the reference point.

If both your and your competitor's offering create a significant amount of value *and* your competitor is priced significantly lower than the value created, you could end up with ROI and NPV financial metrics that seem inordinately high. You, and unfortunately your customer, may look at the business case and say, "There's no way this produces a 150,000% ROI," when in fact it might. Even though the investment delivers very large returns, your ability to price to capture that value is limited by the competitive price.

The flipside of this is when you look at the investment metrics and think, "We are way underpriced, and we are giving away too much of the value." Although that may be the case, it might also be true that you aren't delivering enough incremental value relative to the competitor to sustain a higher price. **If you try to set your price based on the *total* value delivered, and not the *relative* value delivered, you could end up overpriced** *(https://www.roi-selling.com/blog/7-recommended-strategies-for-aligning-pricing-with-customer-value).*

Value pricing compares against the customer's next best alternative, whereas value selling usually compares against the current state, or status quo. This can lead to very high ROI, which can be misleading.

Conclusion

It is easy to confuse value pricing and value selling because they both say and rely on customer value. In the end, although related, they are significantly different. Use value pricing to set your price relative to the competition. Use value selling to justify the investment in your offering based on the price that has been set.

Section 7: Other

Introduction

We started publishing the *Amphora Consulting Blog* the same month that *Grassroots Strategy* was published. While we try to stay focused on the concepts and frameworks explained in the book, we sometimes explore other topics that are relevant to B2B companies.

The topics in this section range from behavioral economics to budgeting to innovation. By the way, we believe that innovation issues at most companies aren't the result of a lack of innovative ideas. More often than not, there are lots of innovative ideas but what companies lack is the ability to recognize those ideas and a disciplined process to vet those ideas in a way that leads to successful business strategies.

In fact, that is a theme across these essays – a disciplined way of thinking about your customers and markets is critical to success. That is why we believe that leveraging the Grassroots Strategy methodology is a powerful way to unlock the innovation potential of your organization.

This section covers a range of topics, so forgive us for the bumpy ride. We hope there are some nuggets that you can use along the way. But most of all, enjoy the journey.

An Unexpected Lesson in Change Management

September 9, 2024

If you were raised even modestly Christian, or know a little about art history, you probably recognize this image as a depiction of the Last Supper. However, if you look closely, you notice something unexpected – amidst the familiar wine and bread, in the center of the table, is a guinea pig!

This painting hangs in the Cathedral Basilica of the Assumption in Cusco, Peru. The Cathedral was completed in 1654, but it took over one hundred years to fill the massive walls with the hundreds of paintings and sculptures required. This particular piece was completed in 1753 by Marcos Zapata, a Peruvian artist and member of the 'Cusco School' – a group committed to teaching European art techniques and themes to local artists.

That Zapata included this local delicacy in his depiction is not a huge surprise. Roasted guinea pig ('Cuy' in indigenous Quechua language) is still a common dish in the Andes. In fact, for many years, roasting a guinea pig was reserved for special occasions, or at least big family dinners at grandma's house. So, while it looks unusual to us (or even disgusting, if you grew up with these furry pets) from that perspective, the mammal's presence makes sense.

What requires a bit more thought is why the Spanish Catholic authorities hung the painting without demanding it to be altered, and have allowed it to stay in the holy place for 270 years! They certainly could have coerced Zapata to change his design – these are, after all, the same church authorities that brought us the Spanish Inquisition – but they didn't. I think the reason they left the painting alone conveys some important lessons about change management.

The big lesson seems to be that change management doesn't stand a chance if you can't make it relevant to those you want to change – Including a celebrated local dish helped communicate the meaning and importance of the imagery to the largely illiterate remnants of the Incas whom the Spanish were trying to convert. In addition to this eternal truth the painting also suggests several less obvious best practices of successful change management:

- Focus on the 'Why?' of the change – Focusing the imagery of the Last Supper on the symbolic invitation to participate in Jesus's saving grace provided the compelling "why" for the locals to convert to Catholicism. This message was much more important than the meal actually served. We have argued previously that the evidence is overwhelming, people are more motivated if they understand the purpose for what they are doing beyond just making more money for the boss.

- Don't let perfection be the enemy of progress – Letting the locals think that Jesus and his disciples dined on guinea pig is not technically correct (it is a new world mammal and would have been unknown in first century CE Jerusalem), but almost irrelevant relative to the larger message. Trying to process map every detail and demanding 100 precent adherence to mandated changes is tempting but can miss the bigger picture.

- Involve those impacted with the 'How?' of the changes – Including those steeped in the local traditions in helping to convey the message and adapt the tactics to their reality was a wise a strategic choice on the part of the Church. In general, including those impacted by change in designing, communicating and implementing change programs can dramatically accelerate buy-in and thereby improve the likelihood of success.

- Balance positive and negative incentives to change – During the time of the Inquisition, hundreds of thousands across Europe showed up for Catholic services and mouthed the litany but continued to practice their 'heretical' religious rituals in secret. Change experts call this phenomenon 'tacit compliance' – It is as If people are saying, "I will do the minimum to keep you off my back, but not change my beliefs, hoping that the next leadership team (or Pope?) will bring a different set of priorities."

  o While it is necessary to have a plan for those who do not adjust to the changes, one needs a balanced approach. The Cusco Last Supper may be an example of a more positive, and potentially more productive approach, to change the hearts and minds of those they were trying to convert.

- Even with a positive message, some people still won't make it – as one of our clients says directly "I give people my expectations, I align their incentives with meeting those objectives and I give them the tools and training to get it done. At some point, if they cannot adjust, we are both better off if they seek employment elsewhere." While it doesn't need to be as harsh as eternal damnation or the tactics of The Spanish Inqusition, without consequences for those who resist, an entire change effort can be lost, as the rest of the organization learns to view change as optional.

- Lastly, a picture really is worth a thousand words – Using The Last Supper, as well as other compelling visual images, has been a key part of communicating the core stories and concepts that comprise the Catholic Faith. In a completely different context, those of us who have been consultants for a long time know the satisfying feeling that comes with nailing the 'killer chart' – a usually simple image that communicates the case for and/or intent of a change. We remember one client where we developed a Venn diagram that summarized the major decision rights for various parts of their organization. They liked it so much that the image became the cover page of their employee handbook. The image simplified and clarified the message for the target audience (unfortunately, over time some employees took to calling it the Mickey Mouse book because of the image's resemblance to Disney's iconic logo, but that may be the price of fame).

Conclusion

While we can't be certain of the reasoning behind the church's decision to hang this painting without alteration (and make other local adaptations to Catholic tradition and imagery) – we can be confident that it worked. Today, 35 percent of Peruvians report attending church at least once a week, while that number is below 20 percent for most of Europe and below 5 percent in Nordic countries and the UK.

Change management is frequently discussed and rarely done well. Perhaps these centuries-old lessons can help you think differently about the challenges of changing your organization – what could happen if you could really reach hearts and minds with the 'why?' and achieve broad engagement? Can you see how these concepts might apply to some of the challenges that you currently face?

Special thanks to longtime friend Ron Bruggeman who unintentionally suggested this blog topic.

Why Do We Make Irrational Economic Decisions in Life and in Business?

March 24, 2020

In B2B buying decisions and consumer purchases, humans do not always make optimal or even rational economic decisions, as predicted by **Rational Choice Theory** *(https://www.investopedia.com/terms/r/rational-choice-theory.asp)*. If this is true, why do we continue to preach value-based selling? The fascinating and evolving study of **Behavioral Economics** *(https://news.uchicago.edu/explainer/what-is-behavioral-economics)* may hold the answers. Behavioral economics uses empirical observation to explain human behavior. Before we discuss the connection to value selling, let's dig a little deeper into the types of decisions that people make in life and in business.

Two Primary Modes of Decision-Making

In his book, ***Thinking, Fast and Slow*** https://www.amazon.com/Thinking-Fast-Slow-Daniel-Kahneman/dp/0374275637), Nobel Laureate economist **Daniel Kahneman** *(https://en.wikipedia.org/wiki/Daniel_Kahneman)* posits that there are two primary modes of thought in decision-making:

- System 1, which is more instinctual, emotional, and quicker.

- System 2, which is more analytical, deliberate, and logical, but is slower.

System 1 Decisions

System 1 decisions are much easier to make, and for many decisions this is probably the best mode. But there are a great many shortcomings, far too many to discuss in this post.

Most significantly, System 1 decisions rely solely on known information and experience. As a result, they do not consider information that might actually contradict the decision. They are also very reliant on emotions and are highly susceptible to overconfidence. Things that should be irrelevant, like sunk cost, factor into what is ultimately a poor decision. In a business environment with a strong push to "get things done," decisions that should be made using a System 2 framework are made quickly through a System 1 quick decision. The results can be disastrous.

System 2 Decisions

In contrast to System 1, System 2 decisions demand stepping back, slowing down, and making decisions based on research, thorough analysis, and a thoughtful evaluation of the options.

On many levels, System 2 should be the primary mode for making any decisions of significance to a business. This framework should also be applied periodically to routine decisions to ensure that they are still the best approach.

It's plain to see why System 2 decisions are much more likely to result in rational economic decisions that benefit an organization.

Business Checks and Balances

Over time, businesses have recognized that too many important decisions were made using a System 1 rather than System 2 process, despite not knowing anything about Kahneman's theory. Recognizing that too many individual, snap decisions negatively impacted business performance led to systems of checks and balances being put into place.

These checks and balances can take many forms, but there are several things most companies of any size have established. The first and most prevalent is that there is an approval process for any significant decision or spending, even if it is already in the budget. The approval process typically includes a cost-justification of the initiative if it involves a significant outlay of money (this could be as low as $10,000).

Some companies have gone so far as to set up a network of "economic evaluators" that are outside of the project and build financial estimates for those projects. Companies have also established "buying committees" that are either standing committees that evaluate projects, or ad hoc committees tasked with evaluating a specific initiative.

These checks and balances have been established to reduce the likelihood that significant decisions are made based primarily with System 1. They also give a framework for making System 2 decisions, which are much harder and require skills and processes that many people either don't have or at least don't practice on a regular basis.

This is Where Value-Based Selling Comes In

Value-based selling processes and tools are designed to help a buyer and seller perform one of the most important parts of a System 2 decision: economic analysis and justification. Economic justification, or the business case, is typically one of the critical components needed to receive approval to move the project forward under the checks and balances that likely exist.

By no means is this meant to downplay the importance of the emotional buy-in of the project sponsor or the project's ability to meet the functional requirements of the business! But these are often not enough to get the green light to move forward. The business case is essential.

Conclusion

Although Behavioral Economics tell us that humans may not always make the best, economically rational decision, even in a business setting, businesses have put measures in place to ensure that good business decisions are made most of the time.

Those measures typically involve an economic analysis of the decision. Value-based selling can help to make it easier, both for your sales team and your customers, to perform an economic analysis that facilitates more approved deals.

This is a Time for Thoughtful Re-Planning

March 24, 2020

Rethinking your plans in light of the unthinkable

To call these times turbulent is an understatement [note the publication date]. Obviously reducing the risk to lives is paramount, but the unprecedented threat of the Covid-19 virus and the necessary response are already wreaking havoc across the economy, with some second and third order effects that may be felt for years. Yet, as bad as things are, it will be behind us one day. The actions companies take today can have a huge impact on how quickly they recover and how they are positioned to succeed when that day comes.

Many companies plan on an annual cycle and then, once plans are finalized, operate as if the goal is 'make the plan at all costs.' This is rarely a sufficient operating ethic (as Enron found out), but extreme circumstances really expose its flaws. A plan is only as good as the assumptions it is based on, and when those assumptions change, the plan needs to adapt.

Unfortunately, this 're-planning' often occurs without the research, preparation and thoughtful cross-functional deliberation that characterize a good planning process. Blunt tools, like across the board cuts, treat the symptoms but rarely address the root causes. 'We need to do something' may be true, but this bias towards action can create long-term problems.

So, as companies prepare for the 'new normal' whenever it arrives, what can they do? From our experience there are a few things that every company should keep in mind:

- **Don't plan based on a point estimate of the future**. Plan around a range of inputs and understand the impact of the drivers that are the most critical. This will allow you to have contingency plans in place for many circumstances (admittedly, maybe not a global pandemic) and enable a more rapid and targeted response.

221

We recall a client in the summer of 2008, where a CEO kicked off their strategic planning process with the advice: "Oil is at $140 per barrel and the experts say it will only go up. I want all your strategic plans to reflect the impact of $200 per barrel oil." Needless to say, this turned out to be horrible advice. Oil prices fell to a low of about $54 per barrel in December of 2008, hovered around $100 per barrel for several years, then fell again into the $40 per barrel range in 2016, and now with both the softening of global demand and the disagreements at OPEC, oil is at

$25 per barrel as of this writing. Worse yet, many of the same experts who said oil prices could 'only go up' are now projecting that they will fall further, with at least one expert suggesting oil prices could actually fall below zero: *https://www.foxbusiness.com/markets/oil-price-could-fall-below-zero-analyst.*

- **Make tactical decisions with an eye to strategy**. Clearly a crisis of this magnitude requires immediate action – much of it unpleasant. Across broad sectors of the economy, we are seeing facilities closed and employees laid off. But even as you make these difficult decisions, you should not abandon your strategy. If you have a clear understanding of your strategic priorities and core differentiating capabilities, for example, you might make different decisions on what investments to maintain, even as you are forced to cut costs elsewhere. Across the board cuts in 'discretionary' spending may meet your short-term needs to control costs, but they are rarely the right answer – if this spending was really discretionary, then why were you planning on it in the first place? A better way to think about this spending is to get to the root causes: why did we think it was a good idea when we budgeted for it and how have those assumptions changed?

- **Sort out the permanent change from the temporary**. The worst will be behind us one day, but whatever world we return to will not be exactly like the one we left. Some of the actions taking place in this crisis will lead to permanent changes, and not all of these are easy to anticipate. In a mild example, some companies may change their work from home policies after learning how to leverage web and video conferencing out of necessity. And who knows what the long-term implications are of 'social distancing.' In a more tangible example, hospitals may change their policies about stockpiling critical protective gear and medical equipment.

We are reminded of the disruptions to air travel following the September 11 tragedy. Most analysts assumed that once Americans regained confidence in airport security that air travel would return to pre-9/11 levels. But they missed the fact that the new security procedures changed how at least some air travelers made trade-offs. As a consultant living in Cleveland at the time, I traveled frequently to Detroit. Prior to September 11th, the way to minimize door-to-door time was to fly, especially for an experienced traveler who was comfortable showing up at the airport after boarding had started. After September 11, longer and less predictable security lines required arriving at the airport significantly earlier. As a result, those of us minimizing the door-to-door time now chose to drive rather than fly. And while overall air travel miles did recover to pre-9/11 levels, this reduction in volume on routes that are a 4–5-hour drive became permanent. Being thoughtful about what might change coming out of the current situation will allow you to plan for the future that will be, not the past that was.

- **Understand the option value of flexibility**. Too often, managers are rewarded, often implicitly, for displaying confidence. But the truth is that the future is always full of uncertainty. Acknowledging this should lead to a preference for actions that maintain or expand our options in the future over those that lock us into a course of action. In the 2008-2009 recession, for example, Honeywell made a corporate decision to manage through the downturn with furloughs, forced unpaid vacations and wage freezes rather than lay-offs. While lots of employees grumbled about the pay cuts at the time, this allowed Honeywell to rebound more quickly than other companies when the recovery occurred, as they did not have to hire or train employees. Understanding that the impact of decisions you make today is not just their short-term financial impact, but the value of the options that

223

they create and/or close-out is critical to crafting your response to this crisis.

Obviously, we don't have all the answers. Every company faces a different situation and the near-term imperative to keep our employees and our communities safe outweighs any financial consideration. But make no mistake, the decisions you are making now have a long-term impact. Making those decisions in the right context and from the right perspective could make all the difference in how you are positioned for the recovery that will come.

Leadership Now and in the New Normal

May 28, 2020

You can't just "follow the science", but don't ignore scientific method.

Decision making in times of unusual uncertainty is one of the greatest, perhaps the single greatest, challenges of leadership. Navigating the current COVID-19 crisis and crafting appropriate responses has been a challenge for leaders around the world. And whatever happens, we are likely to have years of second-guessing as to what we could have done differently. To some extent this is inevitable – with so many unknowns, it is a certainty that we either over-reacted or under-reacted, deploying certain measures either too early or too late; and we may never know which, as we cannot go back in time and try something different.

As we slowly return to some kind of new normal, what lessons can business leaders draw from this situation and its evolving challenges? One piece of advice that has emerged recently is the idea that we just need to 'follow the science.' That sound bite must test well, but it is based on the false choice that we must either follow the science or ignore the science and 'go with our gut.' In truth, no right-thinking person is in favor of ignoring 'the science.' But deciding which science to follow and what actions are indicated remains difficult, as it is during any rapidly evolving crisis in business or elsewhere, for a number of reasons:

- First, scientific certainty takes a long time. In a quickly evolving crisis, action needs to be taken before all the facts are in. This means that we are not dealing with 'settled' science, rather we are dealing with models and projections. And while some of those models have improved dramatically, many were initially fabulously wrong, as models almost always are.

- Second, when it comes to policy, not all scientists agree. At the present time, there are respected doctors arguing that we should extend shut-down orders until a vaccine is found and others suggesting that the health impact of the shutdown (depression, suicide, domestic violence, postponing medical treatment) may actually be worse than the impact of the virus. Further, many individual scientists have changed their minds over time. In the world of science, this is a good thing – when presented with new information, science 'revises its hypotheses.' But this makes it difficult to rely on scientific opinion alone to make long-range decisions.

- Third, scientists are human beings and as such, they are biased. It would be nice to think that because someone has an advanced degree in a scientific discipline, they can look at a set of facts and draw an objective conclusion, but that is not how our brains work. Every one of us, regardless of background or intelligence, makes conclusions based on emotional factors and then 'tells ourselves a story' with selected facts. Selective interpretation of data is part of why well-meaning people disagree on so many things (see "The Righteous Mind" by Jonathan Haidt, for a thorough explanation of this phenomenon and its implications). At a minimum, this means even the 'experts' favor solutions that leverage their particular expertise – so in a complex business situation, no single expert is likely to have the complete perspective.

- Lastly, and closely related to the previous reason, for complicated issues, no single branch of science has all the answers. Complex decisions require trade-offs. So, a decision-maker has to balance contradictory and sometimes seemingly irreconcilable advice. As the current situation highlights, it can be tempting to focus only on the most visible aspects of the crisis. But every decision reflects a cost or a compromise, and sometimes there are second and third order effects that are not immediately evident. For example, as already mentioned, keeping the economy shut down has a personal as well as financial cost. How and when to open up is a challenging question, and no wonder that you might get different recommendations from those who specialize in different aspects of the problem. The same is true in business, leaders need to clearly define objectives, align incentives and coordinate goals to make these dynamic trade-offs over time. Further, they need to recognize that in a crisis, specific goals and targets may need to change as the assumptions underlying them are no longer valid.

So, if you can't just 'follow the science,' what is a leader to do? We have long counseled our clients to follow a hypothesis-driven approach, and that advice hasn't changed. In short, just because individual scientists may be wrong, don't give up on the scientific method.

Scientific method, as you may or may not remember from middle school, is what makes the idea of scientific progress possible. One forms a hypothesis consistent with observable facts, designs an experiment to test that hypothesis and determines if it can be accepted or rejected. After multiple tests, accepted hypotheses become theories (note they are not 'facts' as counterexamples might still surface) and rejected hypotheses get re- formulated for further testing.

In a simple example, if you have a hypothesis that water will boil at a lower temperature at a higher altitude because of the lower atmospheric pressure, you can stash some water and a Bunsen burner into your backpack and climb a mountain to run a test and measure the result.

In business, we have seen broad adoption of the word 'hypothesis,' probably something for which we can thank consultants. But, as one of our clients pointed out, just saying "my hypothesis is…" to mean "well, I think that…" may make you sound smarter but doesn't really change anything. So how should business leaders use this type of thinking, and why is it particularly relevant during a crisis? Here are a few pointers:

1. **Remember hypotheses are not the same as assumptions**. Good hypotheses are consistent with all known facts, so in a rapidly evolving crisis, as the facts change, so should our hypotheses. Many business leaders have been taught to value confidence and hence may state

things as known when they are in fact still uncertain. While in normal times, this may be inspiring, the danger is that it shuts down inquiry and may slow a company's response when their assumptions turn out to be wrong. This may be a really good time to revisit some of your own "everybody knows…" statements, if events haven't already forced you to do so.

2. **Beware of the naive hypothesis**. A naïve hypothesis is an oversimplified explanation based on too little data to be meaningful, often just personal experience. A recent example was seen with spring breakers on the Florida beaches in early March – when interviewed, they said essentially, "I don't know anyone who is sick, therefore this virus must not be a big deal." Just as this turned out to be wrong, when data are changing daily, it is a mistake for leaders to base decisions solely on their personal experience.

3. **Understand that you can't prove a negative**. This is a subtle, but critical, distinction that is broadly relevant in the business world. We remember distinctly a client general manager whose position was, "I know our exclusive distribution strategy is right, we just need to fine-tune it." Our consulting team found out the hard way that it was impossible to prove that the exclusive distribution strategy would not work – every piece of evidence we presented that it was not working (and there was a lot of evidence), was met with a response along the lines of, "we just need to improve execution." Since we could never prove that we had exhaustively tried every possible improvement idea, we could never 'prove' that it wouldn't work. As a footnote, this division president retired shortly after our work and his successor broadened distribution and presided over a three-fold increase in sales. Even this doesn't 'prove' that the exclusive distribution strategy might not have worked, but it seems like a strong indication.

4. **Know when to stop asking for more data**. In a crisis, there are likely lots of things that you would like to know that you cannot know exactly.

But not knowing something exactly doesn't mean you lack insight into the problem. Even with a lot of unknowns, you can often form good hypotheses. For example, one of our clients sold maintenance management software designed to optimize process uptime. While it would take a detailed study to understand how much a particular customer would benefit from their offering, they could make a pretty good estimate based on just a couple of pieces of data (e.g., cost of downtime, value of customer's output, are they running at capacity?) and use that estimate to dramatically improve targeting for their salesforce. Business leaders have to strike a balance, using the data that are available, but resisting the temptation to instinctively ask for more data before making a decision.

5. **Recognize the option value of flexibility**. When you realize that hypotheses may turn out to be false and need to be re-visited, it should be clear that you wouldn't want to lock yourself into positions that are difficult to undo when things change. We experienced this vividly in 2001 as part of a major consulting firm. The consulting industry was already experiencing a downturn by the middle of 2001 and then after September 11 of that year went into a full-fledged crisis: many of our clients froze discretionary spending while they studied the impact on their businesses, and for a while we didn't even know if it would be possible to fly to see our clients. Unfortunately, just prior to that series of events, our firm had implemented a new partner compensation program where pay cuts and demotions were no longer permitted among the partnership. As such, the only way to reduce partner compensation to weather this crisis was to reduce the number of partners, which is exactly what happened. To a certain extent, this made sense, as partners are the most highly compensated individuals in a consulting firm. But partners were also the salesforce, so as the consulting market recovered, our firm was at a disadvantage and lost market share in many critical sectors. In a time of crisis, you should strive to have more degrees of freedom, not fewer.

229

6. **Acknowledge the importance of running 'tests'.** One of the problems with using scientific method to set policy is that sometimes there is no easy way to run a controlled experiment – for example, when the Fed lowers interest rates, there is no way to know what would have happened if they hadn't lowered rates. One way that business leaders can at least partially overcome this is to allow different facilities or regions to try different things, enabling what scientists call "natural experiments.' While not a substitute for a real controlled study, if viewed objectively, this can be a great way to rapidly test multiple responses. But it requires measurement, feedback and a way to share the results. This type of delegation is not weakness, in fact it can be a source of strength. One of the secrets of Wal-Mart's success in the 80's and 90's and Whole Foods Market's success in the 90's and 00's, for example, was a high degree of local store manager autonomy relative to other retailers.

Incorporating scientific method into how you think about your business can be powerful, but it is not easy. Like scientific progress, it starts with recognizing that not everything is known, and further that some of what we think we 'know' may be wrong. Acknowledging the incomplete state of our knowledge, while still taking decisive actions incorporating what is known is the central challenge of crisis management. It will be interesting to see what lesson business leaders learn from the current situation.

What do Innovation, Rock and
Defense Tech have in Common?

April 16, 2020

What do Rock 'n' Roll, innovation and defense technology have in common? If you've heard this story, you probably have a guess. If not, it might surprise you to find the answer is one person: Skunk Baxter.

Jeffrey Allen "Skunk" Baxter (1948 –) is a talented musician, songwriter, producer and sound engineer. Mr. Baxter joined his first band at age 11 and was originally a drummer. He taught himself how to play bass and guitar while in high school and eventually became a proficient keyboard player as well. He played in several bands while at Boston University as a journalism major and worked part-time in a music store repairing guitars and amplifiers.

His professional music career began in the late 1960's as a session guitarist, but his talents were quickly noticed. He was selected to be a founding member of Steely Dan and played on their first two albums. When founders Walter Becker and Donald Fagen decided they would stop touring and only play in the studio, Baxter left Steely Dan and signed on to the Doobie Brothers. In five years recording and touring with the Doobie Brothers he fundamentally altered their sound, both through his guitar-playing and other contributions in the studio, and because he introduced the band to Michael McDonald who replaced original lead singer, Tom Johnston.

McDonald lent his unique vocal style to the band's biggest hits like 'Takin' it to the Streets' and 'What a Fool Believes.' The latter won a Grammy in 1980 for song of the year. After leaving the Doobie Brothers, Baxter continued to be a sought-after musician and producer. He has toured and/or recorded with the likes of Elton John, Linda Ronstadt, Bryan Adams, Eric Clapton, Sheryl Crow and Rod Stewart – a veritable who's who of rock royalty. Baxter still plays today, and in addition to his studio work, writes songs for television shows and movies. Incidentally, he has never publicly disclosed the source of his

231

nickname.

All-in-all, an incredible journey for a multi-talented musical genius. But as you may have guessed, this is only half the story...

In the mid-1980's, Baxter become interested in defense technologies that he might be able to apply to recording music, primarily compression algorithms. With the help of a neighbor who was a retired engineer who had worked on defense contracts, Baxter tracked down data sources (pre-internet), eventually subscribing to 'Aviation Weekly' and 'Defense News.'

Though entirely self-taught, Baxter wrote a white paper on an application for a missile defense system that eventually caught the eye of his congressman who was able to get him in front of the right sub-committees. Adept at explaining complex technologies and their implications in layman's terms, Baxter was granted increasingly higher security clearances and was eventually named Chair of the Civilian Advisory Board for Ballistic Missile Defense.

Today, Baxter serves as a consultant for the DoD and the intelligence community, as well as several major defense contractors.

At first blush, this story seems so fantastic that it almost can't be true, except that it is. While the details are unique, the truth is that this is almost always how innovation happens – someone who is an 'outsider' with no stake in how we've always done things is able to connect the dots in a different way and produce something that is a game-changer. So, at this time when innovation is not just a priority, but a matter of survival to many companies, it is critical to ask, "who is your Skunk Baxter?"

How do you find and leverage people who can think differently and persuade others to think about what could be and not just what has been (or what is in the annual plan)? Based on our experience with our clients, we have developed a list of things many companies overlook that we believe are worth considering:

1. Recognize that innovation is about connectivity at least as much as

discovery – Skunk Baxter has said, "We thought turntables were for playing records until rappers began to use them as instruments, and we thought airplanes were for carrying passengers until terrorists realized they could be used as missiles." In a more relevant example, when Apple introduced the first iPod, all of the hardware technology was at least three years old – a lifetime in consumer electronics. What set the iPod apart and enabled it to define the category was not the hardware, but rather the iTunes 'eco-system' that made downloading and managing digital music legal, easy and fun.

2. Evaluate the idea not the source – too many companies shut down ideas because they didn't come from the right part of the organization. Yet as advertising genius Leo Burnett observed decades ago: "Good ideas don't care where they come from." One of the reasons that Skunk Baxter was able to make his original recommendation on missile defense was that he was essentially adapting a Navy system to an Army application. We can't help but wonder if, without an outside forcing function, the Army might otherwise have rejected the idea as "not invented here." One thing we know about innovation is that you cannot script it or force it to occur on your timeline. By all means you should have a systematic process for evaluating opportunities – we define a pretty good one in Grassroots Strategy – but it should focus on making the idea better, not running down the source.

3. Cherish polymaths – in this complicated world with increasing specialization, it is too easy to assume that there are no longer any polymaths, those who are good at many things. Thomas Jefferson is the classic American example. We know him as a statesman, author and (self-trained) architect, but he also spoke five languages, was one of the first winemakers in the US and played a more than respectable violin. While perhaps rare, polymaths are out there and when you find one, they should be cherished, as people who can look at problems from more than one perspective can bring unique insight. Perhaps you

can start by asking your team what they have a passion for outside of work.

4. Reward integrative, not just functional, thinking – too many companies reward and promote excellence in a function (finance, sales, operations, etc.) without giving people many chances to work across departments. Yet, the answers to complex problems almost always require integrative thinking – not optimizing within one 'silo' but stepping back and thinking differently about the whole. We recall a conversation some years ago with the President of the US for a major global financial institution. Since this gentleman was nearing retirement, someone at the dinner asked him what experience had most shaped him and prepared him for his larger general manager roles. He surprised just about everyone at the table when he said it was a rotational assignment that he had reluctantly accepted to spend 18 months in Human Resources (HR). He said that prior to that assignment, he was comfortable as a 'finance guy' in a finance company, believing that the numbers told the whole story. He learned in HR that there is always a people side of every decision, and he felt strongly that that insight helped set him apart as a general manager.

5. Try periodic creativity breaks – while we are generally skeptical of claims that innovation can be sparked by locking people in a room with Tinker Toys and having them work on problems unrelated to their businesses, there is increasing scientific evidence that innovative ideas typical occur when you are thinking of something else. In other words, innovation cannot be forced. There is something to that instinct that good ideas strike when you are in the shower, or out for a run. So, if you and your team are stuck, take a break. Go to the gym, go bowling, or work on a community service project together. At a minimum, it will be good for you, and you might just find the next big idea popping into your head when you least expect it.

Innovation is unlike anything else that a leadership team has to do. You cannot

234

make it happen on your budget or within your deadline – forcing it to do so ensures that you will only get low risk, incremental ideas. Ordering your team to work harder to innovate without changing the rules or the players is like that paradoxical lyric from "What a Fool Believes": "trying hard to recreate what had yet to be created." Instead of trying to mandate innovation, enlightened leaders will strive to create the environment where innovation can flourish – where opportunities are evaluated on their merits and given time to blossom and grow.

One of the keys to creating a better environment for innovation is being able to recognize and empower your Skunk Baxters. Powerful ideas can come from the unlikeliest sources, are you and your team even looking for them?

Can you make the headache of budgeting a thing of the past?

December 1, 2020

It's that time of year again – no, we are not referring to the holiday displays starting to appear in stores which seems to happen earlier each year as the holiday season gets longer. We are referring to the equally long season of budgeting that is ongoing for many of you reading this. CFO Magazine estimates that the average company spends 32 days on their annual planning and budgeting and worst performing companies spend 56 days or more! And that is just calendar time – when it comes to person-hours and opportunity cost, the reality may be even worse. Some years ago, Ford Motor Company calculated that annual budgeting cost their organization $1.2 billion! And by most accounts, Ford has a better than average finance function.

On top of all this effort, budgets are frequently developed and implemented in ways that drive counter-productive behaviors. Everyone who lives through this process knows that you have to ask for more than you actually need, as cost budgets will get reduced, and sales targets will be increased. Often a tremendous amount of work is done to develop bottom-up budgets that are then completely overridden by top-down 'stretch targets' that not only create re-work at lower levels to make the numbers tie, but sometimes aren't approved until several weeks into the new year.

This is also the time of year when many departments engage in what one of our clients call "fiscal follies." Since budgets usually can't be transferred to other cost centers, department leaders feel that they have to 'spend it or lose it.' This reflex is not driven by cost-benefit analysis, rather it is the fear that not spending will be seen as proof that you really didn't need it in the first place and practically assures that you will be stuck with a lower budget next year.

All of these issues have been well documented over multiple decades and yet budgeting processes have changed very little. A recent client experience highlights the difficulty of changing past practices. We were asked by a long-

Potential Purpose of Budget	Potential Alternatives
• Give earnings guidance to Wall Street – justify and set targets	• Some successful companies do not give guidance • EPS guidance requires macro forecasting, not detailed line-item budgets
• Give the board confidence that we are being aggressive and that we can deliver (see above)	• Does not require detailed line item budgets • Some companies have central strategy groups to analyze trends and potential by business unit
• Unified volume forecasts to coordinate department-level planning	• Requires detailed forecasting (SKU level) for operations, but normally weekly or monthly (not annually) • Best practice is a robust S&OP process
• Spending control for cost centers	• Variable budgets would be more responsive to unplanned changes in volume • Best practice is evolving to parameterized metrics (e.g., IT cost per employee)
• Target-setting for incentive comp	• Need unified targets to commit to board and align functions... • ...But 'bright-line' incentives tend to drive dysfunctional behavior

term client to re-engineer their annual budgeting process. This is not typically work we would pursue, but we were concurrently working on a corporate strategy and the balance of effort between business units and the corporate center was squarely in our scope, especially as all the business units described the corporate requirements around budgeting as one of their pain points.

Sticking to our principle of getting to root causes, we kicked off our first meeting by asking the seemingly innocuous question 'Why do we need budgets?' After a long awkward silence, we eventually had a robust discussion. At our second meeting we had generated a list of possible reasons for budgeting and began to think about alternatives to the current process to achieve these objectives. The client team eagerly engaged in the chance to dramatically change this time-consuming and frustrating process. By the end of that second meeting, we had one camp advocating for a dramatically simplified rolling budget process and a second group that wanted to eliminate budgets altogether.

We were looking forward to the third meeting when we got an email from the client's CFO that the project was being postponed indefinitely. The CFO gruffly informed us that we were wasting too much of his team's time on 'theoretical issues' when he needed them to get busy working on annual budgets! You can't make this stuff up.

So, why do you need budgets? From this work and other experiences, we have come up with a number of reasons and possible alternatives:

We don't claim to know the answer, this list may not even be exhaustive, but we do know that you can't fix a problem without understanding how you got here. And, if this past year has taught us nothing else, it has reinforced that our assumptions are always wrong, sometimes wildly off. Chasing false precision through a detailed budget process may be comfortable because we have always done it that way. But that detail requires a lot of work and does not seem to translate to better business performance. With a little creativity, we are confident that companies can develop compelling alternatives to today's detailed budgets.

We know it is a stretch but imagine a future where every department and individual is making decisions based on the world that we actually experience, not based outdated assumptions made a year ago through a process that we know is broken. Recall that 'framework for making decisions among competing alternatives' is one of our definitions of strategy. How much better could those strategies be if they were developed with the same level of effort and rigor as the current budgets?

Innovation – You Can't Go It Alone

September 8, 2020

Senior innovation leaders confirm that after years of talking about innovation, they are still struggling to integrate customer/market perspectives into the innovation process.

Amphora Consulting recently completed a survey of 20 senior innovation leaders. Our findings support the perspectives shared below. Complete results of the survey can be found here: (https://amphoraconsulting.com/wp-content/uploads/2020/09/Innovation-Survey-Results-2020.pdf)

Innovation is and continues to be a hot topic. There is certainly no shortage of material written on the subject: about 70,000 books by one estimate. And there is no shortage of advice. A recent Harvard Business Review article went so far as to suggest that maybe there was so much baggage that we should stop calling it 'innovation.' More common is the advice to create an innovation leader and charge them with reinvigorating growth. For example, a 2017 article on innovation suggested: "Select one person and give them a clear mandate – and budget – to deliver innovation. When you define their role and empower responsibility, you will deliver results." Yet there is an emerging consensus that this is not a one-person show.

Our recent survey of senior innovation leaders supports this consensus. First of all, the Chief Innovation Officer role is relatively new, in more than half our respondent companies, if the role existed it had been created in 2018 or later. Further, the specific responsibilities and expectations for the role are still in flux, with our respondents reporting very different responsibilities and objectives. Most importantly, the number one reported opportunity for improvement was cross-functional collaboration to drive innovation. While our respondents indicated that their organizations were relatively mature in dealing with the mechanics of tracking innovation, for example, stage-gate and portfolio management; they also reported that integrating customer and market input into innovation continues to be their biggest challenge.

Assuming that putting someone in charge of innovation will yield positive results may indicate a deeper problem in understanding how innovation actually happens. Specifically, we believe the tools and techniques that deliver efficiency improvement have been mastered by most organizations but will never deliver innovation. In fact, the very instincts that many leaders have refined through successful careers will not work, including the tried and true, "if there is something that needs to be improved, put someone in charge of it and hold them accountable for measurable results." This probably explains both the increase in the number of Chief Innovation Officers and their mixed track record thus far.

The reason we feel so strongly about this is summarized in what we have come to call the fundamental paradox of innovation:

> *You cannot order people to come up with better strategic growth ideas and do it on your timetable.*
>
> Or the corollary:
>
> *It is disingenuous to expect someone else to come up with the great idea that you can't come up with yourself.*

Directly from 'Grassroots Strategy':

"This difference bears repeating. You can order someone to turn in their expense report by Friday, and maybe even threaten to withhold their reimbursement check if they don't comply. But you cannot order someone to come up with the next great product idea by the end of the week.

Yet too many companies unwittingly try to force innovation using the management tools and techniques that work in the rest of their business. Invariably, they end up with incremental, low risk ideas and no big wins. Thinking differently and questioning implicit assumptions takes time and, in some organizations, courage. "

Reviewing the survey results, we have become more confident in our assertion that centralizing innovation in one department not only won't work, it may actually do harm because hundreds of smart, creative people now think that innovation is 'someone else's job.' The good news is that the innovation leaders surveyed have come to this same realization. What they are still figuring out, however, is how to rally the rest of the organization to build a culture of innovation.

If traditional management tools of budgets, incentives and deadlines won't work, what will? Well, clearly, there is no magic bullet. Success starts with recognizing that innovation always contains an element of serendipity – the right person being in the right place and connecting the dots in a way that no one has before. While this can't be scripted in advance, you can go a long way by creating the environment where the right kind of interaction is more likely to take place.

This starts with acknowledging the lesson that most companies learned years ago with 'quality.' It is not a department, rather it is a true cross-functional capability. Success requires everyone to realize that it is part of their job. Some suggestions include:

- Define what good innovation looks like using a common vocabulary built on the principles of Grassroots Strategy – make sure that funded innovation projects have a compelling strategic logic, not just a good spreadsheet.

- Broaden where your teams are looking for growth ideas – while many 'ideation' exercises are a waste of time, it is essential that teams break out of incremental, customer-driven product-centric ideas. Make it clear that innovation includes questioning your mix of not only products, but services, delivery channels and business models.

- Encourage cross-functional cooperation and sharing, since no one has a monopoly on good ideas – too many stage-gate processes include a market assessment at gate one and then focus primarily on technical

241

feasibility. In contrast, great innovation requires a two-way dialogue with those in the market and those in the lab communicating continuously as assumptions change.

- Champion innovation across the organization without letting it devolve into a template-driven requirement – many in our survey realized that it is more powerful to make tools and training available and encourage their use than it is to mandate compliance which can lead to a 'check the box' mindset.

- Align existing processes with market-back thinking to inject the customer's perspective throughout the process – you cannot create an innovation culture by ordering it to happen, but all too often existing processes actually discourage the right behaviors. Acknowledge the past and change the processes that are hindering innovation.

- Tolerate failure but not sloppy thinking or repeating avoidable mistakes – one key element is a visible backlog of early-stage project/ideas. At the risk of stating the obvious, no one will offer to kill their project if it means they might not have a job next week. When killing a project is rewarded with the chance to work on an alternative project with higher potential you stand a much better chance of seeing objective go/no go decisions.

For many companies, this is nothing short of a cultural and organizational transformation, and transformations take time. Success requires leaders to practice both patience and humility, characteristics often in short supply in leaders who have built their reputations on confidence, quick decisions, and high expectations. A culture of innovation takes consistent leadership from the very top – even superhuman effort by the best innovation leaders will likely fail if the Board/CEO above them is judging performance only on making the current quarter.

Our advice is to take a deep breath and repeat: "innovation is different." You don't know all the answers, but done well, it is possible to unlock the power of your organization. When we wrote 'Grassroots Strategy,' the analogy of the backyard gardener stuck with us. You can provide the right environment, but you cannot order seeds to grow on your timetable. Leaders would be well served to think about innovation the same way. So, roll up your sleeves, put on your boots and gloves and keep working the soil!

The Adventures of 2023 Planning and Lessons from a Tumultuous 2022

December 22, 2022

By any measure, 2022 was a year of nearly unprecedented change and for many of us, one that we are not in a hurry to see repeated. While 2022 saw most of the covid-related restrictions lifted, experts are still debating the lessons and the long-term cost to things like education and small businesses as well as impacts on mental health. In addition, many businesses are still struggling with covid-related supply chain issues, including supply chain 'whiplash' in industries that saw big spikes in demand.

In the aftermath of the pandemic, pent up demand is keeping many industries strong (have you been through an airport lately?), even while some fundamentals of the economy look weak. Unemployment remains low, but partly because millions have voluntarily left the workforce. Since this summer, we have been experiencing inflation rates higher than we have seen in nearly 40 years. In response, the Fed is rapidly raising interest rates which has industries that depend on capital investment becoming increasingly nervous.

There is a rare consensus among economists and commentators that we have either entered a recession or soon will be in one. Of course, no one knows if it will be short or long, deep or shallow, or how the various factors above will play out industry by industry. All this makes planning for 2023 even more of an adventure. For most of our clients, budgets are tight, contingency plans are being drafted, and, in some cases, the layoffs have already begun.

Reflecting on all this as we do our own planning for 2023 at Amphora, we are reminded of two key principles that we have stated before: first the importance of seeing through the turmoil to sort out the temporary from the permanent changes; and second, having a strategy that is robust enough to survive a range of conditions without fundamental change.

On the first point, we do believe that the last several years have accelerated some changes that will be permanent and mostly for the good. A partial list includes:

- Purpose: Increasing recognition among corporate leaders and boards of the importance of a company having a purpose beyond just making more money for shareholders.

- Employee Engagement: A workforce with a changing hierarchy of internal values, in many cases emphasizing lifestyle options (like work from home), pride in their contributions and ability to make a difference above maximizing financial opportunities.

- Focus and Clarity: Related to that, an increasingly savvy workforce that sees meaningless corporate missions and visions as the cheap window-dressing that they are, and hence eyes new corporate initiatives with skepticism.

- Adaptability: An emphasis on agility and the ability to make 'smart pivots' rather 'sticking to the plan' which places a premium on effective, engaging and inspiring communication and (hopefully) is gradually moving the pendulum towards empowerment and away from central control.

On the topic of having a robust strategy, while we do not claim to be prescient, we take some pride that our mission and strategy have held up well despite all the largely unanticipated change in the world around us. We continue to see opportunities to improve our clients' outcomes as well as change individuals' lives by helping them think strategically.

We have adapted to a shift away from big in-person workshops and have experimented with a number of hybrid delivery models, but the core content has changed little. Our value proposition of a repeatable process to embed strategic thinking while improving real business projects still resonates. And our ability to help strengthen client capabilities by supplementing teams with our experienced consultants and proven frameworks has allowed us to build a viable consulting firm that is unlike any other.

Most importantly, as we enter our twentieth year of operating as Amphora Consulting, we have not had to change our core values. We continue to be committed to:

- Objectivity: consultants can always make money in the short-term by telling companies what they want to hear, but we will never do this, even when that means difficult conversations.

- Root Causes: it is easier for consultants to sell standardized band-aid solutions that treat visible symptoms at least for a while. In contrast, we insist on asking why enough times to ensure that our recommendations developed alongside the client treat the underlying causes and can help achieve lasting success.

- Fun: While we always take our work seriously, too many consultants fall into the trap of taking themselves too seriously, never smiling or laughing in front of the client as if the fate of the world depends on their next PowerPoint chart.

This last point is perhaps the one we are most grateful for. For two decades, we have been lucky enough to work almost exclusively with people that we enjoy being with outside of work. In fact, maintaining an ongoing dialogue with interesting people is so important to us that when covid travel restrictions prevented us from having these discussions at hotel bars, we launched our virtual happy hour series. While we always start with a semi-business- related topic, discussions take on a life of their own and have ventured into time travel, quantum physics, the history of innovation and the facial hair styles of Civil War Generals.

Yes, as we get ready to begin a new year, we are truly fortunate. We have a great team who respects each others' work and enjoys each others' company. We have clients who genuinely appreciate what we can do for their companies and in many cases for their personal development and ultimately for their careers. Some of these clients have even gone to bat for us when budgets got threatened.

So, thank you all for helping to make this an exciting and eventful year. We know that the mix of business, the modes of communication and the delivery models will likely continue to evolve. But we are confident that our core mission and values will survive. We look forward to working with you as we face together the next set of challenges the world throws at us. Best wishes for a peaceful and joyful holiday season and a fulfilling 2023!

Reliving the Glory Days and Boomerang CEO's

March 31, 2023

In case you missed it, Robert Iger returned to the helm as CEO of the Walt Disney Company in November, less than two years after "retiring" in 2021. This makes him the latest in a series of high profile 'boomerang CEOs' who return to their former posts after allegedly leaving it to a successor. Other companies where this has happened include: Dell, Enron, Best Buy, Starbuck's, Yahoo, Procter & Gamble, JC Penney, Bloomberg, Seagate, Apple and Xerox.

Disney performed very well during Mr. Iger's initial 15-year run, and we certainly wish him the best as he navigates Disney's current situation, but history would suggest that the odds are against him. While some highly publicized boomerang CEOs did succeed, like Howard Schultz returning to run Starbuck's or Stephen Jobs returning to Apple, more often than not, they do not.

A 2020 article in the Sloan Management Review looked at 167 such instances at publicly traded companies between 1992 and 2017 and found that, on average, boomerang CEOs underperform other new CEOs by about ten percentage points. This is consistent with an earlier study by the UNC Kenan-Flagler School of Business that found that boomerang CEOs 'significantly underperform' their non-boomerang peers.

So, if it rarely works, why do boards continue to look to the past when changing leadership at the top? The stated reason is often that when this type of transition is required, it is best to turn to someone who can 'hit the ground running.' True enough, an outside CEO would take time to get up to speed and in a real crisis this can be costly. However, we suspect that there are usually other underlying reasons behind the choice:

- Risk aversion – picking the known quantity over other candidates even if they may be a better fit for the current situation may seem less risky.

248

- Volitional narrative – the tendency to personalize performance – "things were great when Bob was here, Bob must be a great leader."

- Golden age fallacy – the tendency to romanticize some former time as the 'golden age' that was clearly superior to today (wonderfully parodied by Woody Allen in "Midnight in Paris")

- Lack of internal candidates – at many big companies, CEO succession is a fairly public tournament. Those who are not chosen may leave to lead other companies rather than stick it out for five to ten years or more before getting their next shot, and this can leave a gap in the chain of succession.

We can understand the temptation to think that a prior CEO could simply pick up where they left off and get the company headed back in the right direction. But why do they seem to struggle? The primary reason is that the company they rejoin is not the same one that they left. Markets and competitors are constantly changing, and if the transition is truly due to a 'crisis,' it is likely that some of the old assumptions have changed and so some of the old instinctive moves will not work. Paul Allaire at Xerox would appear to be an example of this. While the company did very well under his initial tenure, when he returned, he failed to recognize how much competition had shifted to software-based solutions and his tactics grounded in hardware-based competition failed to turn things around.

In addition, bringing back an old CEO can send a negative signal to the company. The implied message of 'we want to go back to the good old days' can undermine succession planning and create rifts in the company culture.

Lastly, we think that there may be another factor at play, roughly equivalent to the statistical concept of 'regression to the mean.' If CEO performance is at least partially due to luck (right place, right time), it would serve to reason that after a great run, a second tenure would be closer to average and therefore not as good as the first term. We can't prove this, but it is consistent with our view that luck plays a bigger role in performance than most executives want to acknowledge (and is far more important than they ever admit in their autobiographies!).

How can companies avoid this temptation to try and relive their glory days by bringing back an old CEO? We have a few thoughts:

- First, and most importantly, identify the root causes of performance issues – what has changed with markets, channels, competition since the last regime? These are issues that should be board-level topics but can get lost in the backward-looking nature of many committees and formal report-outs.

- In keeping with the above, fix the strategy not the person – great leadership is important, but cannot overcome the wrong strategy. Boards need to recognize when assumptions have changed and challenge leadership to update their strategy, rather than personalizing the decision as a performance issue.

- Keep an eye on succession planning. The board should know leaders and their potential a couple levels down – even if there is a true crisis, a 'battlefield promotion' of an internal candidate who is not quite ready sends a much better signal to the organization than bringing back a prior CEO.

- Lastly, consider interim leadership and/or mentoring for leaders who are asked to step up. There are any number of options available that will be seen as temporary and therefore avoid some of the downsides of the back to the past solution.

In summary, looking backwards to a previous successful CEO is tempting, especially when they are a legend (or in some cases, even a founder). But like an aging athlete making one more comeback, it rarely goes well.

Understanding the root causes of performance and avoiding the fallacy of attributing it all to personal performance can help avoid the usually negative consequences of boomerang CEOs.

RACI: Love them or hate them, but used correctly, they can add value

March 3, 2023

After years of documenting key processes, re-writing job descriptions and automating org charts, many organizations still struggle to have clarity and alignment around roles, responsibilities, and authority. This impacts business processes, project execution and day-to-day decisions resulting in frustration, inefficiency and sometimes poor decision-making. We have seen this issue in action with our clients across many industries.

Several years ago, we were working with a major candy manufacturer. One of the key triggers for calling us in was the country president's growing dissatisfaction with his organization's inability to make decisions without bringing problems to him. One example that happened to be on his desk when we talked was a Halloween candy promotion with their biggest retail customer, Walmart. We eventually talked his team through the situation and discovered the core issues – three different managers each thought they should make the final decision, and they could cite their job descriptions to defend their position: The account manager for Walmart who was responsible for "maximizing revenue at his account," the VP of Marketing who was responsible for "maintaining and improving our brand equity across the country" and the CFO who was responsible for "implementing our pricing strategy across channels and key customers."

As one of them lamented to us, "lots of people can say 'no,' but no one is sure who can say 'yes'". This is one of the classic symptoms of unclear accountability and misaligned objectives. So, how do we solve this problem?

One approach for clarifying responsibilities is the RACI Matrix. There is no known inventor of the RACI, however it is documented that it was created some time in the 1950s and was in broad usage by the 1970s. A wide variety of companies have used RACI to simplify complex decisions and processes.

251

The RACI matrix (sometimes called RACI model or RACI chart) shows the different roles and expectations for critical key members assume in current processes, programs, or as part of a project or transformation.

RACI is an acronym that stands for:

- **Responsible**: This is the person or small group that is executing to get the job done. If several people are responsible for a task or activity, it's best to assign one person who's ultimately the lead for the work of the entire group.

- **Accountable (Approver)**: This person approves the work or decision. It's their head on the chopping block if something goes wrong.

- **Consulted**: These people should be consulted before certain work is performed or approved. They are typically subject matter experts.

- **Informed**: These are Stakeholders with no active participation in the project, don't have to be consulted, but must be made aware of updates or decisions. Their input or feedback is generally not needed to keep a project going, but the outcome can have a direct or indirect impact on them.

While RACI has outlived any number of management fads and buzzwords, like any technique it will work only if you use it thoughtfully. The key is collaborative effort – driving a robust discussion to anticipate potential conflicts and then sticking to the agreed upon rules. In fact, we would argue that if you used a different technique (not RACI) to have the robust discussion and stick to the agreed upon rules this would likely still lead your organization to the desired outcome.

Done right, the RACI framework can be a catalyst to get everyone on the same page and provides the structure and direction your team needs to successfully run their key processes and functions. Specifically, a RACI process:

- Clarifies stakeholder roles and expectations.

- Promotes accountability.

- Reduces miscommunication.

- Reduces conflict and inefficiency.

It is important to remember, RACI is a framework not a magic wand. There are many things that RACI won't fix, including faulty strategic thinking, fundamentally misaligned objectives and a dysfunctional culture. If these are the root causes of organizational problems, you will want to fix them before spending the time to develop a RACI matrix.

From our experience, here are 6 keys to using a RACI correctly:

- Focus on decisions, not just tasks: most organizations do a reasonable job of defining responsibility for basic tasks – for many it is simply what your boss asks you to do. But as our example illustrates, it is decisions that involve trade-offs that can cause friction. So, deciding which decisions are in scope of the RACI is key. This tool should not be used to document everything, the value is when there are critical, often time-sensitive decisions to be made and potential confusion around who has what authority. Defining the small number of decisions that give you the right to win is a critical first step.

- Be clear on the difference between responsible and accountable: The best way we have found to clarify this is responsibility is task-oriented and accountability is ownership of the results. Some of our clients go so far as to say that the 'A' stands for 'Approved' in order to highlight this distinction. While the complex and nuanced inputs that lead to a culture of real accountability are beyond the scope of this post (but might make a good blog in the future...), a simple definition is best for now: Accountability should be to the individual who is making the decisions. They have the yes or no authority and veto power, AND they own the outcome whether it is the intended consequences or unintended.

- Be very clear under what circumstances "consulted" means veto power (ideally never) and if possible, define these situations in advance (any decision that the requires signing a long-term lease requires the approval

253

of the legal team). Team members that are consulted have knowledge or a skillset that will inform your decision. The team members give advice but ultimately not responsible to complete the task or make a decision (and then logically should not be accountable for the outcomes either). This is a tough one for many companies, often departments with deep functional expertise like legal, IT or risk management assume that they have veto power, but they typically bear no consequences for the potential lost opportunities.

- Engage the whole team in the development: it is essential that all critical stakeholders work through the RACI together, rather than having one person decide. This gives the team comfort in how the roles were assigned and a better understanding of the goal of a task or decision defined. Healthy disagreement during this process is ok. A robust dialogue ensures that everyone feels as though their voice was heard and builds a common understanding of the intent of what gets captured on paper. And for companies who have been through a lot of change (and who hasn't?), strong leadership is required to prevent RACI from becoming just another 'flavor of the month' initiative that creates work but dies on the vine before driving any meaningful change.

- Use realistic scenarios to test the framework – is this really what we should do when this happens? It is key to spend time drafting scenarios that can be walked through with the complete RACI. For example, if your team constantly has confusion on who gets to make bid/no bid decisions, that would be a great scenario to draft and then walk through when you roll this out. Each scenario should describe a situation, provide an assessment of who needs to be involved in the decision and then most importantly provide an explanation as to why those stakeholders have the role outlined. Don't be surprised if you need to add details; for example, who approves a 'no bid' may be different on a $10,000 bid than on a $1 million bid. The "why" behind the chosen rule is key to a learning and application process.

- Effective Roll-out: It is a safe bet that no one in your organization is waiting for a new RACI chart to tell them what to do tomorrow. To make this a catalyst for change, an effective roll-out is key. Every organization has its own communication approach, it is key to create a communication plan and follow it through. The team that developed the RACI will have a clear understanding of the goal and how it was formed, but for those for whom this is new, they will need time, coaching and follow-through to feel comfortable with using a RACI to inform their decisions. Creating a time and place where those affected can ask tough questions and even propose additional scenarios has proven to be a best practice.

So, how did RACI resolve the issues for our candy client? We started by developing no less than 50 realistic and detailed business scenarios that involved important decisions. We then facilitated a meeting of all the department heads and after reading each scenario asked, "whose decision is this?" In most cases at least two hands were raised in response and frequently it was three people who thought they had the final say. After this shared experience, no one could deny that there was a problem.

Working closely with the team, we then used RACI to track the decision boundaries and inputs that made a single person accountable in nearly all the scenarios we could anticipate, eliminating the need for extensive decisions by committee and escalation for approvals. Importantly, we needed to start by to clarifying objectives and eliminating built-in conflicts, for example: minimizing promotion spend and maximizing market share are fundamentally at odds, there is no natural process to resolve these disputes without escalation.

For example, regarding promotions, after getting agreement that the ultimate goal was incremental profit, we required the marketing lead to clearly define the acceptable parameters for promotions, brand usage, display requirements, etc. – the things that sales people could NOT do, even if a customer asked for it. Then as long as they stayed within these guardrails, account managers could negotiate with confidence and make real time decisions in front of their customers. The only acknowledged exception was if a promotion required a net price that was below the previous minimum in that country, it required approval of the CFO, as setting a new precedent could have an impact beyond that one account.

As this example highlights, RACI is the scorecard – it helps you know when you have finished and can help you communicate what is different, but it is not a substitute for disciplined and creative thinking. Importantly, even after you complete your first RACI, it needs to be a living document. A regular review and communication about the RACI will ensure it provides value to you and your team and evolves as new unanticipated scenarios arise.

While far from a cure-all, done properly, a RACI can improve clarity around the set of decisions and processes to improve business performance and reduce organizational friction.

Corporate Culture: You Don't Know What You Think You Know

March 17, 2021

The list of books and blogs focused on corporate culture is expansive and it is a topic that has been discussed for decades. Why then is culture still one of the top issues leaders seek to address in their organizations? What holds organizations back from being able to develop the culture they are looking for?

We have found the topic of culture is filled with a number of myths and misinformation that impede improvement efforts. And we are not alone, McKinsey estimates that 70 percent of change initiatives fail. Everyone knows that "Culture eats strategy for breakfast" or is it that "Culture eats strategy for lunch"? While Peter Drucker is often credited with being the originator of this statement, research shows that it was first put in print by the Giga International Group in 2000 (Giga was a market research company purchased by Forrester in 2003). The phrase was first attributed to Drucker in 2011, but it remains unclear whether he actually said it.

Maybe that is the lesson for trying to change culture – you can't learn something new without admitting that some of what you thought you knew isn't exactly so. In that spirit, we actually spent some time looking at the research (a partial list of references is included at the end of this post). The list below (bolstered by our own experience) captures what we think we know about corporate culture:

1. **Finding purpose at work matters**. Effective leaders use purpose as a tool to inspire and motivate team members to do their best work, consistently. When you know why you are showing up, day after day, it gives you the focus and motivation to complete the task at hand. Research shows an organization's structure is not what changes a culture from good to great, rather it is the purpose and values that inspires and motivates employees. In the end, when you connect a

role with purpose, you drive a culture of engagement and connection, more consistently tapping into that 'discretionary effort' that is increasingly critical in a knowledge economy.

2. **Psychological safety is required for a healthy culture.** A psychologically safe environment creates the opportunity to express oneself without the risk of harming your career, status or influence in the organization. In fact, in Laura Delizonna's 2017 Harvard Business Review Article, "High-Performing teams Need Psychological Safety. Here's How to Create It," she describes how creating a sense of psychological safety leads to higher levels of engagement, increased motivation, improved learning and overall is a performance enhancer. This is done through creating a culture allowing for risk-taking, for the opportunity to speak one's mind, and for the development of skills to allow for healthy conflict. Too often big company practices, both formal and informal, do the opposite – punishing failure, discouraging conflict and giving credit to individuals not teams.

3. **Incentives matter** While in the long run, a healthy culture is built on intrinsic (job satisfaction) rather than extrinsic (monetary) rewards, we have never seen a successful transformation without the conscious adjustment of incentives. In fact, holding people accountable for the right measures and then empowering them to develop their own means to achieve them can deliver both intrinsic and extrinsic rewards and dramatically accelerate change. Too many leaders fail to understand what really motivates their people on the front lines and fall into the 'they will do what I tell them' trap.

4. **Actions speak louder than words.** Employees look to leaders to see how they behave in times of change to determine how they should respond. Often, they are looking for comfort from the leader and commitment in their actions. When this is done well, a leader creates a culture of trust, with the opportunity to persevere through change. When there is a lack of clarity, leaders provide an opportunity for varied

interpretations. Worse yet, when employees see leaders acting in ways that are inconsistent with the stated strategy, they aren't just confused, they frequently "make things up," inferring the 'real' strategy from the actions they observe. In order to create a healthy culture, you and your leaders need to behave and speak consistently. This drives trust and accountability that will blossom through the organization.

5. **Culture change takes a long time.** Experts agree that cultures cannot be changed overnight. Most organizations experience what we call 'work hardening.' Anyone who has been around for a decade or more has seen dozens of change initiatives and corporate proclamations that come and go with little impact on their day-to-day activities. It is natural for them to think that 'this too shall pass.' Our advice to leaders is to communicate, probably ten times more than you think you should have to, to ensure that your visible actions are 100 percent aligned with your stated strategy and then reward the early adopters who get on board with the change. Unfortunately, getting this right requires patience and humility, qualities too often in short supply among senior leaders.

6. **Culture can exist in smaller groupo.** A good manager can lead by example and either supplement or filter out elements of the broader corporate culture. So, you don't have to wait to be a senior leader, you can contribute immediately to the culture of your own group. While this will likely improve performance and satisfaction, there are some risks. It is important that the positive things you are doing are not seen as at odds with the direction coming from corporate. But if you can create an environment like this from the bottom up, it just might develop enough roots and as employees move to new roles, the culture has a better chance to continually thrive.

There is no doubt that changing corporate culture is a big challenge, but culture is one of the most critical things leaders should focus on, especially if they strive to leave a legacy. Consciously articulating the culture, you want

Section 8: Musings

Introduction

Occasionally, something happens in the outside world that challenges our world view, or allows us to express something in a new way. Whatever the trigger, when these thoughts hit us, we sometimes use the blog to share our insights. While not directly related to our core themes of market-back thinking and business strategy, there are often lessons that we can extract from these seemingly unrelated ideas and events.

On too many occasions, the trigger has been the passing of some larger-than-life figure who has influenced our thinking. Death is always a cause for reflection, reinforcing what Aristotle said, "an unexamined life is not worth living." If we learn nothing else from these giants in their fields at least we should remember to try and live each day to the fullest.

Enjoy our random thoughts and feel free to send us your reactions.

RIP Clayton Christensen

January 29, 2020

One of the most original and influential strategic thinkers of all time, Clayton Christensen, passed away last week at the age of 67. Christensen was a professor at the Harvard Business School, a prolific author, dedicated philanthropist and moral philosopher, as well as being an entrepreneur himself before joining the ranks of academics.

Christensen is credited with inventing the concept of 'Disruptive Innovation,' first in a 1995 Harvard Business Review article, and then more completely in his 1997 book, The Innovator's Dilemma. The Economist has called disruptive innovation 'the most influential business idea of the early 21st century.'

For those not familiar with the concept, the basic premise is simple: in any industry, incremental innovations tend to accrue to the established industry leaders, but disruptive innovations always come from new entrants. To be disruptive, an innovation has to meet three criteria (I am paraphrasing):

1. It starts with what the industry would view as 'low end' customers (sometimes not even in the market)

2. It provides a simple solution to a problem that these customers are already trying to solve

3. It changes the business model, not just the product – in fact, the 'product' is often assembled from pre-existing technologies, like the first iPod.

The concept has been applied across numerous industries, and the impact has been profound. Despite the broad awareness and usage of the term, to my knowledge, no one has produced a counterexample. In fact, the concept has proved so enduring that Christensen spent the last 25 years not modifying it but applying it to specific applications like health care and financial services and re-explaining it to new generations so that the overused term was not mis-used. Most recently, he clarified the original concept in the Harvard Business

Review in 2015.

Christensen towered over other strategic thinkers not only because he stood 6 feet 8 inches tall (his 6' 10" son played basketball at Duke), but because he developed and documented one single principle that has shown to be widely applicable and impossible to refute. His work will stand among the finest examples of what all strategists should strive for: concepts that are elegant in their simplicity and endure even as markets and technologies evolve. We are all better for his giant step forward in strategy as a discipline.

'Flow' … being completely involved in an activity for its own sake

November 17, 2021

A pioneer and leading thinker in the world of positive psychology, Mihaly Csikszentmihalyi, passed away last month at the age of 87 (for anyone who is not a native Hungarian speaker, I have been told that 'MeHigh ChickSentMeHigh' comes pretty close to the proper pronunciation). Csikszentmihalyi's seminal work centered on the concept of 'Flow' a phrase he coined to describe the state of "being completely involved in an activity for its own sake. The ego falls away. Time flies. Every action, movement, and thought follows inevitably from the previous one, like playing jazz. Your whole being is involved, and you're using your skills to the

utmost." His research documented and analyzed these experiences in athletes, artists, musicians and others in all walks of life.

Csikszentmihalyi was the son of a Hungarian diplomat. When the communists took over in 1949, his father refused to pledge allegiance to the party. Two older brothers were later killed at the hand of the Communists, one as a soldier and the other in a prison camp. The remainder of the family was stripped of all their assets and forced into exile. Young Mihalyi moved to Rome and worked to put himself through school, eventually ending up at the University of Chicago where he earned a PhD in Psychology in 1965.

During research for his thesis, Csikszentmihalyi observed that while there were hundreds of classified psychological disorders, there was very little known about what makes people happy. He devoted his career to uncovering and describing the characteristics of experiences where individuals feel good – the field that is now known as 'positive psychology.' After decades of study, he concluded: "Happiness, in fact, is a condition that must be prepared for, cultivated and defended privately by each person. People who learn to control their inner experience will be able to determine the quality of their lives…"

His 1990 book, "Flow: The Psychology of Optimal Experience," is one that we have reread multiple times and have given as a gift to countless friends and colleagues. Achieving flow experiences is critical to happiness and mental health and has broad implications for work as well as life. Designing your life to maximize these experiences can make a huge difference in your attitude and outlook.

Flow experiences are characterized by full immersion in a task creating a feeling of energized focus, involvement and enjoyment in the task itself. People describe a sense of full absorption, in the extreme losing track of temporal concerns – think about the painter who is so absorbed in his work that he forgets to eat or bath for two days, or the rock-climber who takes two hours to ascend 18 inches up the rock face, as she analyzes each potential hand or foot hold to choose an optimal path (or perhaps your teenager playing video games, which sadly have been intentionally designed to create an addictive Flow state).

We have written elsewhere about corporate culture and the importance of intrinsic motivation in tapping into the discretionary effort that is so critical to today's knowledge economy. It turns out that thoughtful companies can provide the prerequisites for Flow experiences which are, by definition, intrinsically motivating – engagement in the task is inherently rewarding and excellence becomes its own goal. Creating an environment where more people achieve Flow at work requires:

- Clear goals and objectives, with some discretion in how those goals are achieved.

- Immediate and unambiguous feedback, allowing real-time adjustment in approach.

- A balance between skill level and perceived challenge (tasks that are too easy induce boredom and those that are too challenging produce anxiety – both these have a negative impact on performance).

Clearly all of these have implications for organizational design, and many of you can think about corporate policies that undermine these attributes. In his later work, Csikszentmihalyi focused on this connection, summarizing his findings in a 2004 paper co-authored with Kathryn Britton: "Flow isn't just valuable to individuals; it also contributes to organizational goals. For example, frequent experiences of flow at work lead to higher productivity, innovation, and employee development."

Those who regularly read these blogs know that we like concepts that are elegant in their simplicity, broadly applicable and verifiable – Flow fits all those characteristics. As one example, there is a segment of the population that never reports experiencing Flow. While small, this segment is dramatically over-represented in the populations of prisons and mental institutions, reinforcing that periodic Flow experiences are critical for a stable and mentally healthy life.

Mihaly Csikszentmihalyi had lots of reasons to think about unhappiness and could have added volumes to the study of psychological disorders. But instead, he chose to focus on what makes a positive experience and that has made a huge difference. We are all better off because of this simple yet powerful concept. Cheers to a life well-spent!

What Lessons Can We Take from This Turbulent Year?

December 19, 2021

The end of the year is always a time to take stock of where you are and think about how you might adjust your plans for the future. Even if you are normally not one to make new year's resolutions, this past year certainly must have caused you to stop and reflect.

Many pundits have weighed in on the long-term impact of masks, lockdowns, and social distancing. And the jury is still out on what the 'new normal' will be – which changes in how we work and interact will be temporary and which will be permanent? Add to that the speculation on how long the current inflation will last and when our stressed and disrupted supply chains might begin to function more predictably, and you can drive yourself mad with fright over what the future might hold.

Rather than add my voice to this noise, and try to predict the future, my intention in this post is to look back and try and draw out some underlying lessons from this crazy time and how we might apply them in our lives and careers. You may recall that in September of this year I rode my bicycle across the **country** (https://www.linkedin.com/pulse/stage-twenty-seven-metter-tybee-island-ga-jeff-bennett/?trackingId=iHYIZE1IXXdBZabTezu%2B6g%3D%3D). With seven-plus hours per day in the saddle, I certainly had plenty of time for reflection.

Since returning I have tried to organize my mind's meanderings, and have extracted these five keys principles that the craziness of the last year (including the self-inflicted craziness of riding 2,900 miles in 27 days) reinforced for me.

1. The power of purpose – When times got tough on my bike, one of the things that kept me going was remembering 'why' I was doing it in the first place. Not only was I fulfilling a bucket list item that I had been thinking about for nearly 40 years, but I was raising money to help the children of my late friend, Fred Dillemuth, who was killed in a bicycling **accident** (https://www.gofundme.com/f/fred-dillemuth-memorial-fund). When I started to suffer and feel sorry for myself during some of the more challenging sections, it was as if Fred was riding beside me saying, 'you got this.'

A ton of evidence suggests that the same is true in the corporate world. When people understand that they are working for a higher purpose, they make better trade-offs and give more discretionary effort than when they are just striving to 'make the quarter.' Over time, companies that understand this attract and retain better people and outperform their competition.

If you are not fortunate enough to work for one of those companies with a clear purpose, you can still put this lesson to work. Try to think of objectives for yourself and your team that are linked to some purpose beyond your department goals. Celebrate it when a team member goes the extra mile or earns a new accreditation. By linking your plans and actions to some 'greater good,' you can tap into the power of purpose for your team.

2. The importance of relationships – On the bike trip, those people who had not found a compatible riding buddy by the third or fourth day were generally still riding by themselves In the third and fourth week. The riders that formed teams worked more efficiently and helped each other finish each day's ride. For those that did not, it was a lonely, difficult and potentially dangerous, way to spend day after day on a bike.

The same is true in the office. Most professionals spend more than a third of their waking hours at work (or doing zoom meetings from home). This time can be miserable if you don't have colleagues that you can relate to and have a little fun with once in a while. Further, appreciating the people you work with encourages collaboration and makes it more natural to cover for one another, improving the effectiveness of the whole team.

So, make some friends at work – don't be afraid to reflect a bit of personality and share your thoughts and challenges from time to time. I remember distinctly an initial meeting with a client team where the Senior Partner was describing the internal politics of the client and positioning our objectives. Trying to lighten the mood a bit, I said at one point, "this reminds me of a Brady Bunch episode." My attempt at levity was met by a round of cold stares from the rest of the team. They were all about my age and had grown up in the U.S. – they had to have seen the show (and some could probably tell you that Ann B. Davis played Alice the maid), but they felt that admitting it showed professional weakness. I knew that this was going to be a tough client engagement, and my fear proved to be justified. Long hours need not be drudgery, but they will be if you are not willing to laugh at yourself and talk to your colleagues about something other than the task at hand.

3. The importance of big goals – I have been an avid cyclist for more than 20 years, but I trained in a more focused way for about 18 months prior to this trip – averaging nearly 15 hours per week on the bike over that stretch, while managing to keep the rest of my life together (more or less). Lon Haldeman, the long distance cycling legend who led our tour group has observed that the enjoyment of this type of experience arrives in three phases: first, the satisfaction of training and seeing yourself improve; second, the enjoyment of the experience itself – living in the moment as all you think about is the ride (and how far is the next rest stop!); and third, the enjoyment afterwards, as you can look back on the accomplishment and take pride in what you have done.

All of this translates into a work environment as well. Others have written about the importance of seemingly impossible goals or 'BHAGS.' A clear strategy plays a big role in this. In a world increasingly oriented towards management by short-term measures and mechanisms we lose our line of sight to the power of having the organization aligned around a clear purpose and strategy.

But you don't have to wait for an enlightened leader to declare a target in order to put this to work. Challenge yourself – take on something that makes you a little uncomfortable, volunteer for a role that stretches your functional background or forces you to learn new skills. Author Bob Bitchin summarized this insight by saying, 'the difference between an adventure and an ordeal is attitude.' Embrace this principle and you can achieve incredible things, while enjoying all three phases of the effort.

4. Keep going when things get tough – In cycling up a steep hill there comes a point where you run out of gears – you can't downshift anymore, it is you vs. the mountain. No amount of complaining or even stopping will make the task easier. You have to suck it up and do it (and most importantly, don't stop pedaling because you will roll backwards!).

Many people discovered this insight during the COVID crisis as well – you can complain about lockdowns and restrictions, or you can adapt and do what you can remotely, even if that means extra work to communicate and hold the team together (or zoom calls at crazy hours to accommodate other time zones).

In a different context, I recall painfully learning this lesson years ago in consulting – the deadline doesn't go away, even if someone else doesn't deliver. More than once, I had to work past midnight to type in data myself because the client had provided a file in the wrong format and all I had was a paper copy. I could whine that data entry was beneath me, or I could grind it out and get the work done, recalling that clients pay us for answers not excuses.

You can help your team apply this lesson as well. If the overall challenge seems daunting (and it will if you have set a big goal!), break it into individual tasks with interim milestones. The momentum gained by achieving these milestones will give your team the confidence that they can keep going and 'make it to the top.'

5. Practice gratitude and humility – One huge lesson from the bike trip was just how much of what happens is outside of your control. In four weeks, we saw strong riders who had trained incredibly hard miss sections of the ride because of extreme heat, steep hills, crashes and saddle sores. We don't like to admit it, but luck plays a big role in our achievements. While proud of what I did over those four weeks, and suffering my share of setbacks, I am grateful that none of that misfortune prevented me from finishing.

In the corporate world, we tend to personalize accomplishments and underplay the role of luck in achievement – 'that division blew away its numbers, the leader must be brilliant.' The real world is far more complicated – there are mediocre leaders atop large companies and very capable ones who never get recognized because they are in the wrong division or geography.

In our strategy work, we call this concept, 'the momentum of the business' – a clear and objective picture of where the business is headed if you just continue to gradually improve the things you already do. Separating the impact of market level headwinds and tailwinds is necessary to provide an honest baseline upon which to build a strategy.

The world would be a better place if we all recognized that our success is not just a function of ourselves (nor is failure ever completely our fault) and were grateful for all the good fortune that we have been blessed with throughout our lives and careers.

On that note, I would like to end this post and this year by expressing my gratitude for the people that make what I have accomplished possible. At the top of list is my wife, who not only tolerated, but encouraged my training and my time away from her for the trip. But this trip would also not have been possible without the wonderful Amphora team who held down the fort in my absence and used incredible discretion in resolving potential issues without distracting me during the ride.

In the end, however, none of this would be possible without our clients. We are grateful for those of you who believe in the value of our process and continue to use our concepts and our services year after year, in several cases across multiple companies. Without your loyalty and support there would be no Amphora Consulting (and no money for a long bike trip). And without your understanding, respect and friendship, our work would be a lot less rewarding.

Thank you all and very best wishes for a fulfilling, and hopefully less tumultuous, 2022!

Rest in Peace, Vin Scully, There Will Never Be Another One Like You

August 10, 2022

Baseball broadcasting legend Vincent Edward 'Vin' Scully passed away last week at the age of 94. He was the voice of the Dodgers for an incredible 67 seasons, from 1950 to 2016. The awards and accolades that Scully received during his career are too numerous to mention. As one example, he received the Ford Frick Award for lifetime achievement in broadcasting excellence from the National Baseball Hall of Fame in 1982, and then went on to work for 34 more years!

Scully's longevity stands as a testimony to our concept of focusing on a core capability and not swaying with every fad and passing trend – the Amphora theme of 'strategies that endure.' And it is difficult to comprehend the amount of change that Scully witnessed. He followed the Dodgers from Brooklyn to Los Angeles (in 1958), and transitioned from radio to television, though his style changed very little. He started at a time when baseball was still struggling with integration – he did not actually broadcast Jackie Robinson's first game (as implied in the recent movie), but he did call hundreds of Jackie's games and watched as other teams gradually followed the Dodgers lead and broke the color barrier.

Beyond that, in 1950, there were only 16 major league teams with none farther west than St. Louis. By 2016 only 9 of these were still in their original hometowns, and through four waves of expansion, an additional 14 teams had been added. In 1950, there was no free agency, no designated hitter, no jumbotrons and no players from Latin America, not to mention Japan or Korea. Further, for most of his early years, Scully worked alone in the booth – not flanked by 'color commentators' as is common today and not supported by an analyst feeding him statistics to bolster his narration. Amidst all this change, Scully was the constant, for nearly everyone alive, the only 'voice of the

Dodgers' they can remember.

In addition to his job with the Dodgers, for nearly twenty years Scully worked for NBC Sports, covering golf and football, but baseball remained his true calling. Scully covered an amazing 25 worlds series; his first was in 1953, and he remains the youngest ever to do so. And while he can't take credit for the famous call of Bobby Thompson's home run for the Giants in 1951 play-off game (it was Russ Hodges who said, "The Giants win the pennant, the Giants win the pennant, the Giants win the pennant"), he was in the next booth, calling the game for the losing Dodgers. It is Scully's voice you hear in the replay of Kirk Gibson's pinch hit home run in game one of the 1988 World Series – "in a year that has been so improbable, the impossible has happened."

In a profession where others were known for hyperbole, histrionics and off-the-field antics (or in the case of the Cubs' Harry Caray, all three), Scully was simply a master of his craft. Despite living in a city where celebrity sightings are a daily occurrence, he kept a relatively low profile.

Perhaps the call that best exemplifies Scully's enduring talent is his play by play of **Sandy Koufax's perfect game in 1965** (https://www.latimes.com/sports/story/2022-08-02/vin-scully-sandy-koufax-perfect-game).

As the game nears its dramatic ending, we see Scully's gifts at their fullest. The differentiators that kept him at the top of his craft for over more than six decades:

- Like Hemmingway, he describes details in precise yet uncomplicated words that create a vivid picture of the scene – "Koufax wipes the sweat from his brow with his index finger, then wipes it on his left pant leg."

- He puts the game situation in context, stepping back to remind us why it matters. In the Koufax call, he repeats the time and date, as if to say, "remember where you are right now so you can tell your grandchildren about this historic moment."

- Lastly, he did not need to fill every second with his own voice. In the Koufax call, after the final strike, he is silent for 37 seconds, letting the crowd noise tell the story and making you feel like you were there. This is perhaps why, while the official attendance that night was just over 29,000 people, decades later hundreds of thousands of Angelenos 'remember' being at that game.

Sadly, for baseball fans, the sport no longer means what it did in the Norman Rockwell America where Scully got his start. With its long season and slow pace, baseball rewards patience and perspective and has struggled to keep its audience in the Tik Tok era. Baseball may need to continue changing to stay relevant, but it will never have a better soundtrack than the golden tones of Vin Scully.

We cannot summarize the difference he made any better than Stan Kasten, the President of the Los Angeles Dodgers: "Vin Scully was one of the greatest voices in all of sports. He was a giant of a man, not only as a broadcaster, but as a humanitarian. He loved people. He loved life. He loved baseball and the Dodgers. And he loved his family. His voice will always be heard and etched in all of our minds forever." Rest in Peace, Vin Scully, there will never be another one like you.

Business Travel...Can you really stay healthy?

March 9, 2023

Here it is March, and for most of us our New Year's resolutions have faded in the rearview mirror. Yet as we adjust to a post-Covid world, many would like to avoid returning to old bad habits. In particular, as business travel rebounds to near historic levels, fellow road warriors struggle to maintain a healthy balance.

No matter what your goals or resolutions are, having a healthy approach to business travel is key to ensuring it doesn't negatively impact your health, stress and effectiveness at work. At Amphora, we take the work we do seriously, but also believe that it is critical to invest time to take care of ourselves.

After decades of travel, learning from our mistakes and listening to pointers from others, we have compiled a list of a few simple tips that might make your travel just a little bit less stressful and perhaps a bit more rewarding.

- Never turn on the TV in the hotel room. Leave the remote exactly where you found it. We got this advice years ago from a full-time consultant who was also an age-group competitive triathlete – to keep up his training regimen, he had to use his time wisely. His tip is helpful for a few reasons. It ensures you don't get hooked on some marathon TV show and end up staying up too late. Leaving the TV off gives you the gift of time to check in at home, take a few minutes to stretch or meditate but most importantly doing something that will rejuvenate you, not drain you. Save your binge watching for a weekend night when you don't have to set your alarm clock.

- No matter what your parents told you growing up, there is no glory in being a part of the clean plate club. Typically, restaurant meal portions are meant for people eating out once per week. If you are eating out three meals a day for four or five days in a row, you are clearly consuming too many calories. Again, no one is watching you at that hotel restaurant – you don't need to finish your meal. Order something you wouldn't make at home, taste everything, but do not feel like you have to finish it.

- Be especially wary of the business group dinner – you know what we mean, the whole team gathers at a steakhouse where the average portion size is already more calories than you should consume in an entire day. After a couple rounds of cocktails someone order 'apps' for the table – it should not surprise you that there is nothing redeeming about mozzarella sticks, potato skins of bacon-wrapped shrimp (except that they taste so good!). If this type of dinner is a once-a-year celebration, that is great – if you are doing this regularly, watch out. It will catch up with you!

- Move your body. Schedule the time for your morning or evening exercise. Even 20 minutes can get your blood flowing and just make you feel better about your day. Even if your hotel does not have a gym, get out and walk or do yoga or core exercises in your room. It is important to not feel guilty about taking this time! A regular fitness routine can make you more productive at work. There is increasing evidence that regular exercise supports healthy brain function! That time away from your desk can make you more productive behind it.

- Watch the empty office calories. We continue to be surprised at the number of offices where doughnuts in meetings and birthday cake in the break room are common occurrences. Like any other treat, these are great once in a while, especially if you skipped breakfast. But if you are indulging in these treats in addition to three meals a day, don't be surprised when your pants feel a bit tight. Further, your productivity may be impacted by the energy highs and lows you feel throughout the day with these unhealthy sugar infusions.

- On a related note, you might want to carry a couple of granola/protein bars, fruit, or other semi-healthy snacks in your backpack. Inevitably, hunger will strike when you are running through an airport, and while their food choices have improved somewhat, it is still mainly fast-food quality (the word "quality" used loosely here). Taking a snack from your own stash can save you empty and unhealthy choices.

- While it pains us to say it, be especially mindful of liquid calories; they can add up quickly. Liquid calories come in so many forms, soda, specialty coffee, and alcohol are just a few areas to keep your eye on. More than one colleague has struggled to say 'no' to the question 'one more round?' Our advice is to leave peer pressure in college and recognize that you won't miss much by leaving others to close the bar. And speaking from personal experience, we guarantee that you will feel better the following morning!

- Lastly, don't let deliverables and deadlines turn you into a hermit. We recall an exit interview with a summer intern years ago. Offhandedly, we remarked on how team dinners and interaction with colleagues outside of work was one of the little joys of life on the road. For contrast, we said "if you just work 8am to 8pm and then have room service in your hotel room, this is the worst job in the world." We could see the color leaving her face as we said that, so we weren't totally surprised when she replied, "you just described my entire summer." We were not shocked to hear shortly thereafter that she had chosen not to come back to the firm full time. Humans are social beings. All work and no play doesn't just "make Jack a dull boy," it leads to a dull and ultimately unfulfilling life. So, find time to socialize, meet people, talk about things besides work, it will make your time on the road more interesting and more bearable.

When people talk about work/life balance, it often conjures images of work-from-home, leave policies, free bagels and meditation rooms. For those of us who travel regularly for work it is more about consciously maintaining a healthy lifestyle while balancing the pressures and frustrations of life on the road. It starts with awareness of the choices you are making and then making small adjustments that make a big difference over time.

We know that many reading this are fellow road warriors.

Printed in the USA
CPSIA information can be obtained
at www.ICGtesting.com
LVHW020206241124
797243LV00010B/344